I'm an analytical, left-brained male who set out to give this book a cursory glance and found myself weeping through several stories. I was deeply moved in my spirit, and the suffering represented in these pages stirred a compassion within me that I'll not soon forget. Over and over, the themes evolved from despair to hope, despair to hope. I would happily recommend this book to anyone who ministers to women.

—BRUCE L. KOTILA
Director, Lutheran Evangelistic Movement
Pastor, Thanksgiving! Lutheran Church, Omaha, NE

Read it. Share it. Someone you know *needs* this book.

—JULIE BARNHILL
Author, *One Tough Mother*

In *Starting From Scratch When You're Single Again*, women will find hope, help, humor, and some lovely stories and recipes wrapped in much encouragement for their journey.

—CHERI FULLER
Author, *The One Year Women's Friendship Devotional*,
A Busy Woman's Guide to Prayer, and other books

In 1977, with the sweep of a pen and the hammering of a gavel, I lost my husband, my home, my security, my sense of identity, and my dog. At church I was just as helpless. There were no Single Again classes—for *any* reason. I was a nuisance—a question-riddled nuisance—in the one place and around the very people with whom I should have found comfort. I would have given anything for a book such as this one. It is an incredible reminder of God's grace and purpose for our lives, and it has delicious recipes to boot!

—EVA MARIE EVERSON
Coauthor, The Potluck Club Series and
The Potluck Catering Club Series

D0391265

Starting From Scratch When You're Single Again is a book long overdue. If you have experienced the death of your marriage, then you know, or at least feel, that it would have been easier to die yourself. Sharon Knudson and Mary Fran Heitzman have captured the hearts and the pain of twenty-three women and have woven their stories into a prayer shawl that begins to warm the soul and heal the pain. They connect people with our Lord and His healing power. You must read this book and give one to someone you know who has walked this road of sorrow. There is healing in store for you.

—BOB COTTINGHAM
Senior Pastor, North Heights Lutheran Church
St. Paul, MN

Starting From Scratch When You're Single Again is an encouragement to anyone starting life anew after the loss of their life partner—whether through death or divorce. Filled with humorous and often touching stories, you'll think each story is the best until you read the next one. I was startled by how entertaining this book was, and my wife loved it. Speaking from a purely selfish level, the recipes are a nice addition!

—RICK JOHNSON
Author, *The Man Whisperer: Speaking Your
Man's Language to Bring Out His Best*
Founder and Executive Director, Better Dads

Instead of page after page of advice, this book is filled with page after page of hope. It's stories that allow the reader to learn from real women who were willing to share how God helped them turn from sorrow and move toward their futures.

—JANE KISE, EDD
Author, *LifeKeys: Discover Who You Are*

In this fast-paced, success-oriented world, becoming single again can leave you empty. *Starting From Scratch When You're Single Again* offers warmth and wisdom through women who have been there. Whether you are single again or know someone who is, the nuggets of wisdom, fun recipes, and rich stories will leave you more than full. You'll want to linger over this banquet.

—JEAN BEARDEN
Senior Director, Spiritual Formation
North Heights Lutheran Church, St. Paul, MN

Starting From Scratch When You're Single Again offers countless recipes of hope and healing for brokenhearted women. While unabashedly transparent, this collection of true stories gives an entrance into something greater than life's losses—a place where tragedy and sorrow draw the love of God in exceeding measure and surprising ways. You can't help but feel the come-alongside comfort from this group of resilient women.

—SUSAN D. HILL
Author, *Closer Than Your Skin*

This book is comfort food—rich, tasteful, nutritious, and easy on the heart. Cookbooks come a dime a dozen and mostly end their lives in garage sale boxes. *Starting From Scratch When You're Single Again* is a keeper! The recipes accent a story feast of loves lost and hopes reborn. Sharon Knudson and Mary Fran Heitzman trace their own tales of sorrow and restoration and are transparent and truthful without approaching dark. You'll find the mix both tender and biblically grounded. Jesus is preparing a feast for the end of all things, and here is a worthy appetizer. Taste and see that the Lord is good!

—MARK HERRINGSHAW, PhD
Pastor, North Heights Lutheran Church
Coauthor, *Six Prayers God Always Answers*
and *Nine Ways God Always Speaks*

This delightful collection of stories, lightly peppered with Bible verses offering God's promises, is sure to bring hope and inspiration to those who have lost their spouses. I love the "Guiding Principles" that follow each story and provide advice gleaned directly from the experiences. All that and mouthwatering recipes too. This book is sure to be a hit!

—CONNIE LOUNSBURY
Contributor to *Guideposts*, other magazines,
and short-story book collections
Coauthor, *Reaching Past the Wire: A Nurse at Abu Ghraib*

Miracles are abundant in *Starting From Scratch When You're Single Again*, a collection of true-life stories of twenty-three women who learned to thrive while stirring the bitter batter of life's hardships, challenges, and crises following the death of a marriage. In delightful cookbook format, hope and encouragement are the main ingredients served up by this practical guide to healing. You'll crave a double batch!

—DEBORA M. COTY
Author, *Smiles to Go Before I Sleep: Hugs, Humor,*
and Hope for Harried Moms

In their delightful and creative new book, *Starting From Scratch When You're Single Again*, authors Sharon Knudson and Mary Fran Heitzman offer hope and encouragement to those who have experienced life's sorrows. Each chapter gives a personal story, unlimited encouragement, practical advice, and even a favorite recipe to anyone experiencing, or who has previously experienced, the death of a marriage or the death of a spouse. With stories, words, advice, and much more, Sharon and Mary Fran—themselves the victims of sorrow—uplift and inspire others who walk a similar path. I highly recommend this book.

—DENISE GEORGE
Author, *What Women Wish Pastors Knew*

Thought-provoking, pain-filled, hopeful, and real. This book shows perseverance, rescue, and faithfulness through stories of emotion that everyone needs to read when in a state of singleness.

—CHERYL SCRUGGS
Hope Matters Marriage Ministries, Inc.
Author, *I Do . . . Again*

For women who find themselves divorced or widowed, these stories offer inspiration, comfort, and practical ideas for rebuilding your life. Each beautifully constructed chapter begged me to pause for prayer.

—NANCY JO SULLIVAN
Author, *Moments of Grace, Did You Get What You Prayed For?*
and *My Sister, My Friend*
Cocompiler and Editor, *Stories for the Heart*

If you have lost a spouse through death or divorce and longed for someone to understand the depth of your pain, read *Starting From Scratch When You're Single Again*. Authors Sharon Knudson and Mary Fran Heitzman share women's stories—including their own—of unimaginable loss and eventual healing. Poignant, tragic, humorous, yet always memorable. You'll find a reason to hope again.

—Joan C. Webb
Speaker/Teacher/Trainer, Life Coach, IW LifePlan Facilitator
Author, *The Relief of Imperfection: For Women Who Try Too Hard to Make It Just Right* and *The Intentional Woman: A Guide to Experiencing the Power of Your Story*

Just because you're divorced or widowed doesn't mean it's the end of your life. Statistically, we know that most people marry again. The stories and guiding principles in this book can serve to equip people so they are less apt to make the same mistakes twice. *Starting From Scratch When You're Single Again* shows how to heal and move on, but also proves that keeping God central in marriage—and every area of your life—is key.

—Wilfred G. Sager, EdD
Retired Marriage and Family Therapist
Founder, Sanctus Marriage Enrichment Ministries

Starting From Scratch
WHEN YOU'RE
Single Again

SHARON M. KNUDSON
MARY FRAN HEITZMAN

Christian
LIFE
A STRANG COMPANY

STARTING FROM SCRATCH WHEN YOU'RE SINGLE AGAIN
by Sharon M. Knudson and Mary Fran Heitzman
Published by Christian Life
A Strang Company
600 Rinehart Road
Lake Mary, Florida 32746
www.strangdirect.com

Design Director: Bill Johnson
Cover Designer: Judith McKittrick

Published in association with the literary agency of WordServe Literary Group, Ltd., 10152 S. Knoll Circle, Highlands Ranch, Colorado, 80130.

Library of Congress Cataloging-in-Publication Data:
An application to register this book for cataloging has been submitted to the Library of Congress.
International Standard Book Number: 978-1-59979-254-5

NOTE: All of the incidents in this book are true. Some of the names and locations have been changed to protect the privacy of the individuals involved.

First Edition

08 09 10 11 12 — 9 8 7 6 5 4 3 2 1
Printed in the United States of America

Dedication

To Bob…my rock.

Walking with you is an adventure, and you've
enriched my life beyond measure.

Love,
Sharon

To Duff…you're the best.

Thanks for your patience, encouragement, and hours
of quiet time.

Love,
Mary Fran

Acknowledgments

To the twenty-one other women in this book—thank you for sharing your stories with such grace and transparency. Your persevering faith in a loving, miracle-working God strengthens the rest of us for whatever may come our way.

Greg Johnson, our agent at WordServe Literary—your idea launched this project, and your advice always came at just the right time.

Jessie Nilo, our "reader extraordinaire"—your excellent and thorough critiques, tempered with sweetness, cheered us on.

The Strang Communications team—Donna Hilton and Debbie Marrie, you are truly a pleasure to work with and an encouragement to us as first-time authors. We benefited not only from your expertise, but also from your enthusiasm about Starting From Scratch's potential ministry.

Mary Fran's family: Suzie, Chris, Max, Abby, Kristin, John, Grant, Kate, Sam, and Bobby—you encouraged me and waited patiently for me to rejoin our social life.

Sharon's family: JoEllen, Jessie, Dominic, Alicia, Jared, Janae, Susie, and, of course, Mom and Dad—you taste-tested these recipes and listened to the stories behind them.

Mary Fran's neighborhood critique group: Cathy Buechele, Jeannette Burns, Peg Fling, Jeanne Lickteig, and Julie Murnan—you've listened to and encouraged my writing for many years.

THE MINNESOTA CHRISTIAN WRITERS GUILD—learning from you is invaluable, and the networking opportunities are priceless. Without your influence, we wouldn't be writers.

OUR EXTENDED FAMILY AND CLOSE CHRISTIAN FRIENDS—you prayed for us again and again, keeping God's presence and creativity in the equation. Thank you for your countless prayers that held us up and carried us forward.

OUR LORD—You're always with us to lead and to guide, perhaps even more so when we're starting from scratch.

Contents

Foreword

ONE OF THE KEY ISSUES I HAVE EMPHASIZED DURING MY years as the voice of HomeWord is the devastating effect death and divorce have, especially on women. Everyone around them is affected, and if they have children, the ramifications often set the entire family spinning out of control.

Sharon and Mary Fran have sought out women who not only came through their ordeal but also flourished despite incredible odds. They did extensive interviews of real women instead of making their book yet another compilation of stories. By doing so, they captured the real essence of pain and chronicled how it was lived out and overcome. It's obvious from their writing that they've walked similar paths themselves and want to help other women on their journey.

This book is like a compendium of advice for what to do when disaster strikes. Themes such as depending on God to enter fully into your experience and standing firm against bitterness reverberate. Sharon and Mary Fran remind us to pray fervently, welcoming the Lord fully into experiences that can otherwise overwhelm. "Take good care of yourself," they say, "and above all, know that you have a big God who is capable of using all things for the good of His children." To paraphrase Scripture:

> God is able to do immeasurably more than all we can ask or imagine, and after this season of suffering, Christ Himself will restore you and make you strong, firm, and

steadfast. He lifts up those who are bowed down and heals the brokenhearted.

—FROM ROMANS 8:28; EPHESIANS 3:20;
1 PETER 5:10; PSALM 146–147

With the divorce rate in our country now approaching 60 percent and an aging population that will no doubt see an increase in the number of spousal deaths, *Starting From Scratch When You're Single Again* is poised to meet the needs of many. It reveals intimate experiences from women of various ages and locations in a variety of settings and circumstances. Yet the bottom line is always the same: trust God. He will not let you down.

—Dr. Jim Burns
President of HomeWord
Author and radio host (www.homeword.com)

Introduction

YOU ARE HOLDING HOPE AND ENCOURAGEMENT IN YOUR HANDS. This book carries the voices of twenty-three women who, in one way or another, have lived through the death of a marriage and yet found peace, forgiveness, and hope for the future. Read how God walked with them during their darkest hours. Their experiences resound with the message that you can get through the grief, you can get past the rejection, and you can grow strong. Not only will you survive, but you will also thrive!

The two of us (Sharon and Mary Fran) have ourselves lived through the devastation of divorce or death of a loved one. We know how utterly bereft it can make you feel. Together we have gathered these true stories from women ranging in ages from their early twenties to late seventies. We sat at many dining room tables, relaxed on living room sofas, and perched on kitchen stools. When time and distance prevented personal meetings, women's hearts and stories were shared over three-way phone calls.

We have laughed and cried together. We feasted on chocolate cake and strawberry desserts. We wrapped our hands around cups of hot tea and tall glasses of icy water. Each story brought with it a personal picture of strength, resilience, and amazing faith. Now you too can meet these women. They have loved and lost, grown strong through adversity, and come through victorious with the help of God.

Many times during the process, we prayed for each woman by name. We thanked God for her willingness to share her particular heartache, knowing that her story would touch others who are living through similar trials. From the beginning, we gave this project to

God so that He would bless it and allow us to touch many lives with hope and encouragement.

Maybe you will recognize yourself in one of these stories, or perhaps recognize someone who is experiencing similar trials. If a story resonates with you, embrace the hope it offers. If it sounds like the trials of a loved one, share the hope with them.

Finally, since some of the stories include facts about men who physically or mentally abused their wives, we want to assure you that this book in no way is a man-bashing forum that suggests all men are bad and all women are good. As you will see, many women who shared their stories have been uplifted by wonderful men in their lives—spouses, friends, pastors, and relatives—who were a blessing from God.

May these stories encourage you and give you hope. No matter how lonely you feel at this moment, no matter how meager your resources, with God's help you can rebuild your life, even if you are *starting from scratch.*

One

Stir With Faith

GOING THROUGH LIFE IS MUCH LIKE STIRRING. WHEN A mixture of ingredients is thrown into our bowl, we stir in ever-widening circles, watching as they cohere and form a batter. When the heat is turned up in our lives, we must "stir constantly" so that nothing burns at the bottom or boils over and makes a mess. *Faith* is an action word too. When we watch and pray, diligently directing every problem and triumph to God, He is faithful to help us.

The following story titled "Telling" comes out of an experience Sharon Knudson recorded in her journal. It alludes to the guilt and shame she felt after she fought hard to save her marriage and failed. When she runs into a church friend at a Christian bookstore, she is so bothered by their conversation that she can't even sleep.

In the "Who Needs God?" story, Kendra Jockety's mother is forced to absorb a twofold loss when both her husband and twenty-one-year-old son die only weeks apart. She was a farmwife at the time and faced hard decisions that affected her family and the farm.

Jennifer Silvera faced disaster when her policeman husband was killed in the line of duty. Only thirty-two years old and with two small children, she is forced to proceed in life without him. "Be Here Now" was his motto, and it became Jennifer's impetus for tackling her future as a single mother.

Will we cling to the Lord when crisis hits, or will we let those fiery trials destroy our faith? Courage is a definite requirement, and sheer bravery is needed at times. But if we will stir and keep on stirring, if we will believe that despite everything God is there, He will see our distress and act on our behalf. Then, as we rejoice in our own transformations, our hearty stew will nurture others, and God will be glorified beyond measure.

Telling...

A conversation with Sharon

Be merciful to me, O Lord, for I am in distress; my eyes grow weak with sorrow, my soul and my body with grief.
—Psalm 31:9

Bedtime—how I dread it. It reminds me that I am utterly alone.

I pile several books and my Bible on *his* side of the bed, hoping to somehow diminish the sense of the vacancy there. It does help a little. Lifting the covers, I climb between the powder-blue sheets and arrange three large pillows behind me. "You nestle into the covers like a cat," my husband used to tell me. It's at night when I miss him the most, when the thoughts I have kept at bay during the day start shouting and become impossible to control.

Reading the Bible helps, so I open to the Psalms and chew on a few. I underline and highlight a few verses. I draw stars and teardrops in the margins.

I'll journal tonight, I decide. It helps to put things in perspective. In fact, I'll write about seeing Lisa Hayes at the Christian bookstore today. It was extremely awkward, and I can't get it out of my mind.

And so I begin.

> *Oh, no! You see me and head my direction, smiling. We haven't seen each other for a long time, and you have no idea of the tragedy in my life. You might ask me how my husband is. What will I say? How will I start?*
>
> *"You haven't heard?" or maybe just, "We're not together anymore." Or how about, "Our thirty-year marriage just ended. It's a terrible thing." I would rather keep it a secret— no explanations, no history of events, no words spoken, no hint of my devastation interlaced with shame.*
>
> *But that wouldn't be fair to you, would it? You knew us as a solid, forever couple. We smiled in public, went to church, led Bible studies, and showed just the right amount of relationship. No one would have guessed there was a crisis in our home.*
>
> *So now I have to watch your face change from a smiley, "Hello, so nice to see you," to palpable shock and disbelief. You won't know what to ask, and I won't know what to tell you. "Say as little as possible," I think to myself. I know you admire him—maybe more than you admire me.*
>
> *Yes, your world will be rocked by this furnace blast of truth, and you might even think, "If it can happen to them, it could happen to me." And then, despite everything I have suffered, you will want me to comfort you.*

"Grief work is exhausting," I tell myself as I change my position in bed. I set my pen and journal aside so I can tuck myself in under the quilts. I have discovered that a person needs several blankets when they sleep alone.

5

It must be getting late. I have been journaling for a long time. I crank my neck to look at the clock, and the red neon numbers tell me it's after midnight. I wish I could sleep, but there is no use trying yet—not with my mind still obsessing about today.

Lisa and I once went to the same church, but she moved away. A few years later I also stopped attending that church—too embarrassed to face people after the divorce. My husband and I had been members for more than ten years. Established as leaders, we had multitudes of friends. He taught adult classes, and our kids attended Sunday school and youth group. I was the music director, among other things, and over the years the choir grew in number from thirteen to thirty-eight.

But everything changed when the news hit that we were getting a divorce. If a bomb had exploded in the center of the sanctuary, it would not have been more of a shock. People were incredulous, and rightly so. We never let on that there was trouble. We had not dared; it wasn't the acceptable thing to do.

I have since taken a job as organist in another church because I desperately need the money. That means I'm committed on Sundays, and it's just as well. Not that anyone would have gossiped or thought ill of us. Their concern is genuine, but they have no way of knowing what is true and what isn't.

And perhaps I'm a little paranoid too. I think of the psalm that says, "If an enemy were insulting me, I could endure it; if a foe were raising himself against me, I could hide from him. But it is you, a man like myself, my companion, my close friend, with whom I once enjoyed sweet fellowship as we walked with the throng at the house of God" (Ps. 55:12–14).

Telling is perhaps the hardest thing a person who is going through a divorce has to do. No doubt it is difficult for the widowed too. It is one thing to cope with the trauma, but having to inform your friends adds another whole level of excruciating pain. Someone should write a book about what people go through when they suddenly find themselves alone.

I glance at the clock again. It's 1:00 a.m., and sleep still eludes me. Did I just lose a whole hour staring into space? Evidently.

I close my Bible and with a loving caress, hug it to my chest. There has been a physical ache inside me for months, and holding my threadbare Bible close feels like getting a heart massage—as if the words within are warm, alive, and medicinal. "It's not a cliché," I tell myself. "God's Word really does soothe the weary soul." I decide to sleep with my Bible again tonight.

But I'm still wide-awake. Maybe I'll get sleepy if I write some more. So I pick up my journal and retrieve the pen from the folds of the thick blue bedspread. OK, where was I? Oh, yes...Lisa.

"You are a dear friend," I say to Lisa, "but I haven't told very many people. Please don't be offended that I didn't call."

She still will not be dissuaded, and she forces me to give her an explanation. As I speak, I wonder how much I say is too much. Do I sound bitter...angry...resentful? Do I appear unreasonable or wrong...crazy, out of whack? Is my narration believable—or not?

The more I say, the worse it sounds. How little can I tell and still pass your exam?

After a while, I stop talking and look down at my feet. You stare at me long and hard, and you look as if you're wondering many things. I must hurry to a conclusion, I decide. I need to be done with this recital. Remembering has made me feel dreadful—my stomach hurts, my mouth is dry, my knees are wobbling, and I can tell the blood has drained from my face. It will take several hours before I feel normal again.

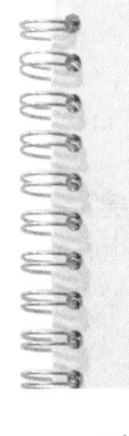

I stumble to an end and hope I said enough. I wonder if I have shown the right amount of grief. Do I dare let you see how I am beginning to heal? Probably not.

We say good-bye, and as you leave, I become aware that I wrecked your cheery mood. You walk away toward the checkout near the door. As you go, I wonder what judgments you will decree... whom you will tell... what you will say.

There! I got that out of my system and onto the page. It feels good.

I glance at the clock and see it's 2:30 a.m. No wonder I'm tired! I lean over, turn off the light, and get cozy under the covers.

"Thank You for getting me through the day, Lord," I whisper over and over to Him. I pray myself to sleep.

Guiding Principles

A Pinch of Salt

> Read Scripture, read Scripture, read Scripture. Cling to God's truth, and revel in His comforting love. "Come to me, all you who are weary and burdened, and I will give you rest. Take my yoke upon you and learn from me, for I am gentle and humble in heart, and you will find rest for your souls. For my yoke is easy and my burden is light" (Matt. 11:28–30).

> Journal, journal, journal. It's very therapeutic to get your thoughts and feelings out of your head and onto

the page. "Cast all your anxiety on him because he cares for you" (1 Pet. 5:7).

> ➤ Be careful whom you tell about your situation. Try not to get swept away by your emotions and say things that should be kept private.

> ➤ Ask God to forgive you for places where you failed during your marriage. None of us are perfect, even if we like our friends to believe that we are. In turn, guard your former husband's reputation, and be careful what you say about him. We are to forgive others in the same way that we have been forgiven. "If you forgive those who sin against you, your heavenly Father will forgive you. But if you refuse to forgive others, your Father will not forgive your sins" (Matt. 6:14–15, NLT).

> ➤ If you are the friend of someone who is grieving, be careful not to grill them for details. Offer understanding and unconditional love instead. In the case of divorce, don't make judgments about who was right and who was wrong. (Life usually isn't that simple, and it only leads to gossip.) Offer your condolences and specific assistance if it's needed in some way. And remember to pray for your grieving friends; they need it!

Homemade With Heart

One of Sharon's Favorite Recipes

A warm bowl of soup is the perfect solution if you don't have much of an appetite. During the months I was grieving, I often ate soup. It's easy to make, reasonable in cost, and nutritious. This recipe is quick because you don't have to chop any vegetables, and since it makes a large batch, you can freeze some for later.

Savory Vegetable Stew

1 Tbsp. olive oil
1 Tbsp. minced garlic
2 lbs. stew meat (or round steak)
2 qts. V8 100% Vegetable Juice (low sodium)
1 pkg. (16 oz.) frozen vegetables
    (such as carrots, green beans, mixed garden vegetables)
2 cans (15 oz.) diced potatoes, drained
    (or peel and dice 3–4 medium potatoes)
1 envelope dry beef-onion soup mix
1 Tbsp. dried parsley
¼ tsp. crushed red pepper (optional)
Black pepper to taste

Heat olive oil and garlic in a six-quart saucepan. Cut stew meat (or round steak) into one-inch cubes and add to saucepan. Sauté until meat is brown.

Add the remaining ingredients to the meat mixture. Bring to a boil. Cover and simmer for 3–4 hours, stirring occasionally. Serve hot with crusty bread.

Freeze portions in small containers for later use.

Now for an Update

With a Cherry on Top

While keeping a journal, Sharon discovered she liked to write. She joined a writers' group and started publishing articles in Christian newsletters and magazines. Despite her previously held belief that the stigma of divorce would ruin any future plans for serving God, she has a speaking and writing ministry today that offers help and encouragement to many. Sharon is very active in her church in deliverance and marriage ministries and is past president of the Minnesota Christian Writers Guild. Visit her Web site at www.sharonknudson.com.

Sharon has two grown daughters, three grandchildren, and a wonderful son-in-law. Her story called "Those Cherry Macaroons" (see chapter 6) talks about the unexpected way that God blessed her with a husband. Now God is using her days of "telling" to help and strengthen others.

Who Needs God?

A conversation with Kendra Jockety

> Her children rise up and bless her....
> —PROVERBS 31:28, NASU

If God doesn't care about our family, why should I care about Him? I stared at the guardian angels in my church's stained glass window. Where were the angels a month ago when my brother drowned? Where were they last week when my dad took his own life? Where was God then?

A little boy squirmed next to me, and I heard the pastor say, "The service is ended. Go in peace." I twisted the bulletin in my hands, grabbed my purse, and slid out of the pew. Mom was ahead of me.

I hung back as friends surrounded her with hugs and kind words: "Meg, we're so sorry. How are you doing?" She nodded without saying anything and accepted their condolences. I could hardly bear to look at her. Mom's body had crumpled at the news of my brother's death, and now with my dad's passing, she looked smaller and more fragile each day.

I knew more challenges lay ahead. How long would she hold up? But at sixteen, my immature faith was little help. My thoughts were filled with, "I'm finished with God. No more church for me." I wanted to shake my fist in the face of the Almighty.

After the crowd thinned, we headed to the farm where a stack of blank thank-you notes lay on the kitchen table. Mom wanted to express appreciation to neighbors who had carried in their big electric fans to cool the midsummer heat. She wanted to thank relatives and friends who filled the kitchen table with casseroles, cakes, and coffee in those early numbing days.

Before we sat down to write, Mom put a pot of coffee on the stove, but its usual rich aroma was little comfort for the new grief that had come to live with us. My aunts joined us later that afternoon to address envelopes and lick stamps. It was a good thing they came. I was very little help to my mom, and I was relieved that their busy conversation allowed me to drift into my own thoughts.

Earlier in the week, I walked through the house to look for my mother. As I went from room to room I called, "Mom!" but she didn't answer. The sun shone through the windows, but the house felt dark. I felt dark. The whole world felt dark.

I checked upstairs. There Mom sat in a corner of the bedroom; she had a crumpled tissue in her hand, and her eyes were swollen and pink. I wanted to say something to make her feel better. But I didn't know of any words that could fix the misery of losing a twenty-one-year-old son and husband in the span of twenty-nine days.

I missed them too. We called my brother "Bear," a nickname that fit his dark hair and brown eyes. I lost my appetite when he died, and I dropped ten pounds in twenty-one days. *If only I could see him one more time.*

I thought about Daddy too, and even though his depression clouded many of my memories, I hung on to the good times. I remembered all the days I had walked down the road to the field to meet him in the middle of the afternoon. Summer sausage sandwiches, chocolate cake, and a fruit jar full of lemonade were stuffed into the tin lunch box I carried for him. I always hoped he would notice me on his first turn as he tilled the soil across the long rows of corn.

When he saw me, he stopped the tractor and I ran to where he waited, eager to show him what Mom and I had packed for his lunch. After spending hours in the dusty field, Dad was ready for a long swig of lemonade. He unwrapped the waxed paper from the sandwiches and teased me between bites.

Finally, after the cake was eaten came the event I waited for. Daddy sat me onto the cultivator and pushed a little lever. The part of the dusty red machine I was perched on rose and dropped several times. Having Daddy to myself and riding the cultivator was the highlight of my day. But I knew that my up-and-down ride and the bushy whisker kiss that followed were the signal that it was time for him to resume work and for me to walk the hardpacked field road home.

Season after season Daddy worked the fields and milked the cows. He had always provided well for us, including a life insurance policy he left for Mom. Still, I worried about all the financial decisions that needed to be made. My fragile faith buckled, and I didn't trust God to direct us through the maze that lay ahead.

My aunts' chatter swirled around the kitchen as I reflected on the afternoon when Bear died. I could still see our pastor as he approached the house. Mom had walked out to greet him. With his hand on her shoulder he said, "I'm sorry to bring this bad news. The sheriff's office called and told me that your son drowned a few hours ago at Fish Lake." He added that Bear's body had not been found but that recovery operations were under way.

Mom clapped a hand over her mouth, shook her head, and struggled to stay standing. "Oh, no, no," she said. Daddy was in a hospital sixty miles away, fighting a bout of depression. Arrangements were made to go get him and bring him home.

When I went to bed that first awful night, I didn't know how to pray. How could I say, "Please, God, help the divers find my brother so that we can have his funeral," when my heart said, "Please, God, don't let my brother be dead"? I decided to pray that I would wake up in the morning to find the day's events had been a nightmare.

But God hadn't reversed reality when I awoke the next morning from a troubled sleep. My brother had not miraculously slipped into his bed in the next room. Twelve more hours passed before divers found his body pinned under a log at the bottom of the lake. News of Bear's death broke my dad's will to live. Less than a month after Bear drowned, Daddy climbed to the hayloft, found a rope, and ended his lifelong fight against depression. For decades he fought a valiant battle and embraced the bright days as best he could. But when the oppressive clouds of the dark days moved in and over-shadowed him, I knew I didn't need to feel embarrassment or shame about his death. My memory of him would not be a picture of futility but instead a lasting image of determination and strength.

Chairs slid across the linoleum and broke into my somber thoughts. All the thank-you cards had been addressed. My aunts said their good-byes and headed home to their waiting families.

When the following Sunday rolled around, I wondered what Mom would do. How would she react to this dreariness of not having Bear and Daddy around? If she announced, "We're not going to church anymore," or if she stayed in bed all morning, I could say, "Aha, God! See what You've done? If my mother has given up on You…"

But even before I got up I could hear Mom in the kitchen. I joined her at the breakfast table where we asked God to bless our food— a mechanical prayer for me. After we finished, Mom went to the bedroom to get dressed for church. "How can I tell her I'm not going?" I wondered. I didn't have the nerve to say, "I'm finished with God!"

When my brother died, my faith had been tested, but it survived; now the shock of Daddy's suicide was more than my spirit could absorb.

I got dressed and took the car keys from the hook on the cupboard. I would go to church. I would sit in the pew. I would go through the motions. And no one would see the grudge I held against God.

But that day and through the months that followed, I never heard my mother express anger toward God. She often cried, but she had an inner strength that nurtured my depleted faith.

Over the next few months I adapted to change. While Mom prayed and made decisions, we lived in flux and faced new challenges. Little by little she moved us through the fog of uncertainty. She relied on my uncles for advice. She rented out the farmhouse and some of the land, and we moved to a tiny apartment in town. She took a job at a dry-cleaning establishment where she learned to run a cash register and greeted customers with a cheery hello.

As much as possible, we kept ourselves busy and surrounded by family and friends. Although Mom had always been a caregiver, she learned to receive. One day my aunt called and said, "I'm going to Colorado on vacation. Let your mom know so she can think about joining me."

"Well, I suppose I could get a little time off work," Mom said when I told her about the opportunity to get away. She made sure everything was taken care of at home, packed her suitcase, and took a break from her responsibilities.

When Mom returned, she began to accept more invitations. Sometimes she met friends for coffee or a game of cards. She encouraged me to spend time with cousins and girlfriends.

Eventually Mom sold several acres of farmland. Then she announced, "We're going to build a house." I could hear the excitement in her voice, and I looked forward to the opportunity to keep busy with something new and exciting. We planned and made decisions about size, function, and cost. The rooms on the blueprints were smaller than those of the farmhouse, but the kitchen was still large and allowed extended family to gather in comfort.

One night when the house was under construction, we drove to another town to buy special tiles for the bathroom. On the way home we got lost. Since Mom had never learned how to drive, I was behind the wheel. "Which way is the highway?" I asked.

"I don't know," Mom answered. "I wasn't paying attention."

After an hour of bumbling indecision about which way to turn and how to go back, we giggled and giggled about our adventure. That laughter felt good because there had been so little of it since the two funerals.

Healing came in tiny steps for us. Sometimes we ventured out when we felt like staying home. We spoke my brother's name tentatively at first, and then we spoke it more boldly. We laughed about Daddy's attempts to impress us when he stood on his head or picked up a hundred-pound sack of grain with his teeth.

Somehow we got through all the firsts: the first Christmas without them, the first New Year, their birthdays, and all the other reminders that two chairs were empty at the table. In the first days of grief, I had prayed to get through one hour at a time. Eventually my spiritual stamina grew, and I asked God for the strength to get through a day, and then a week. I was grateful that my trust in God had survived.

Six years after that terrible summer, when I was engaged to be married, Mom surprised me. "Teach me to drive," she said. She had never driven in her life! Now at age fifty-seven, she wanted to expand her independence and learn something new. I wondered if she was bold enough to share the streets with roaring traffic and thrill-seeking teenagers.

I hid my reservations and said, "OK, let's go!"

Mom was nervous from the start. When I said, "Turn left," she would turn right. When I said, "Turn right," she would turn left. I wondered if this was really a good idea.

After several weeks of patience (for both of us), Mom set the appointment for the driver's exam. I knew her blood pressure would soar as she sat in a car with a uniformed highway patrolman. She knew he would analyze her turns, her signals, and every decision she made.

"Just try to relax," I told her.

She failed the test—twice.

But she was determined. The third time she passed! And although learning to drive was a minor event compared to surviving the death of two loved ones, I suspect she depended on God to get her through that trauma too.

I never told Mom that I almost threw God out of my life or that her example had helped me hang on to Him. I'm not sure why I didn't tell her. Maybe I thought if I said, "I'm angry at God," it would have been too harsh for her gentle spirit. Mom didn't talk much about her faith—she just lived it. And her quiet presence was the best sermon I ever received.

Guiding Principles

A Pinch of Salt

> Cry when you need to; laugh when you can.

> Allow others to give you their gifts of time. Accept vacation invitations, kind notes in your mailbox, and listening ears.

> Focus on your strengths, and let God cover your weakness. "Strength and dignity are her clothing, and she smiles at the future" (Prov. 31:25, NASU).

> Dare to learn a new skill, even if you think you can't.

> Take care of yourself so that your children can learn from your survival skills.

> Put your trust in God. "The widow who is really in need and left all alone puts her hope in God and continues night and day to pray and to ask God for help" (1 Tim. 5:5).

Homemade With Heart

One of Kendra's Favorite Recipes

Growing up, I craved date-filled cookies the way other people loved chocolate chip or sugar cookies. Mom made them for me on special occasions like my birthday or during those forlorn teenage years when she sensed I needed an emotional pick-me-up. Even though her stoic German heritage was uncomfortable with profuse emotion, those cookies always said, "I love you," loud and clear.

Mom's Date-filled Cookies

3 cups flour	1 tsp. baking soda
2 tsp. cream of tartar	Pinch of salt
1 cup butter	2 eggs
1 cup sugar	1 tsp. vanilla
1½ cups chopped dates	¼ cup sugar
1 cup hot water	1 Tbsp. flour

Sift together first four dry ingredients. Using a pastry blender (or a large fork), cut butter into dry ingredient mixture.

In a separate bowl, beat eggs, sugar, and vanilla until frothy. Then combine the liquid and the dry ingredients. Mix well.

Refrigerate for at least two hours.

Remove dough from refrigerator and roll out using a rolling pin. Cut into circle shapes.

Combine remaining ingredients in a kettle. Cook until thickened, then cool.

After the date mixture has cooled, place a spoonful on a circle of dough. Top with another circle of dough and crimp the edges together.

Place on a cookie sheet and bake at 350°F for 10–12 minutes, until lightly browned.

Now for an Update

With a Cherry on Top

Following her mother's example, Kendra continued to pray and attend church, but she envied people who had a deep faith. Twenty years after she wanted to "throw God out the window," she asked Him to take charge of her life. She found that relying on God doesn't erase her problems—sometimes it doesn't even offer solutions she can see—but it does provide a sense of peace that she didn't have until she gave up control.

Kendra and her husband, Griff, have been married for thirty-seven years and have three grown daughters and four grandchildren. They work side by side in their family business, where they meet with many women who are widowed or divorced—women who must start life over from scratch.

Kendra's mother remained single for twenty-five years, continuing to set a gentle example of faith before she left this earthly life and took up residence in heaven.

Be Here Now

A conversation with Jennifer Silvera

> My grace is sufficient for you, for my power is made perfect in weakness.
>
> —2 CORINTHIANS 12:9

A single knock brought me to the door. Looking out, I saw three police officers standing shoulder to shoulder with dread covering their faces. Slowly I laid my hand on the doorknob, knowing I didn't want to turn it. If I opened that door, my world would never again be the same.

And I was right.

They had come to tell me that my husband, Shawn, had been killed. Also a policeman, Shawn had been trying to capture a runaway fugitive who led police on a high-speed chase. Shawn had put Stop Sticks down across the freeway, but when the man saw the tire-deflating devices, he swerved and intentionally struck Shawn down.

We were both thirty-two, and life had been good. We grew up together, had a storybook wedding, and then established our careers—he as a policeman, I as human resources director for Hilton Hotels. Together we served two years in Honduras with the Peace Corps and then came home to start our family. When the tragic news came, our two sweet children were playing upstairs—Jordan, a year and a half old, and Madelynn (Maddi), five months. Now both were suddenly without a daddy.

Shawn was a special man who lived in the moment and reminded others to do the same. He was a very involved father, always coming up with new (sometimes comical) child-rearing strategies to try. He brought me flowers every month on the date of our wedding day and made sure my energy wasn't totally depleted by the kids. The vision of what our family was and would be had suddenly come to an end.

Shawn's friends quickly established a Web site as a memorial tribute using several of the photographs Shawn had taken of our family, our time in Honduras, and nature. A whole community of friends and relatives gathered around the kids and me. Journaling became my greatest therapy, but it was not something I had time to do very often with all the other demands on my life—besides managing the grief. Then a girlfriend suggested I use the Web site to journal in a blog. It would be my daily *assignment* to write, and I would be more likely to get it done. Not only would I have my therapeutic outlet, but also I would have a record of experiences to share with the kids when they were older, and hopefully I'd be able to help others all at the same time.

I lived in a time warp without Shawn. Months passed, largely devoid of traditional family times. For two years I stood by myself at the kitchen island with my toddlers propped on barstools—me dancing between them as I coordinated the meal, cleaning up as I went along, and polishing off a to-do list or two. Maybe not sitting at the table made it easier to ignore the hurt caused by Shawn's absence. Yet, mealtime was important, and Maddi and Jordan would never know that unless I showed them.

One night I instructed Maddi, now an endearing two-year-old, to set the table. With enthusiasm, she put out enough forks for seven people. She kept counting and planning where everyone would sit and finally had a eureka moment that we only needed silverware for three!

Three-year-old Jordan was in charge of filling the water glasses. He strained to concentrate, trying not to spill. Without thinking, I sat down in Shawn's old chair. "No!" I thought, and started to get up.

Then another thought made me pause: "Someone needs to lead our children through the meal, and that someone is me."

The children must have sensed it was a special night because when they finished eating, they politely asked to be excused and cleared their dinner plates. "Wait," I said. "Dinner isn't over yet. We're having a celebration!"

"What are we going to do?" asked Jordan, clearly surprised.

"We're going to roast marshmallows over our candle," I told them in the most excited tone of voice I could muster.

Maddi brought out three clean forks, and we each took one along with a marshmallow from the bag. We held them over the candle in the middle of the table, and I used the time to talk about patience and roasting marshmallows slowly so they wouldn't burn. It was a lesson in discovering that all good things come to those who wait.

Then I discussed fire safety and reiterated how only moms, grandmas and grandpas, or other adults are able to light candles and that fires can be dangerous. Jordan agreed. "I need to be safe with fire or my dad would need to fly down from heaven and check on me," he said in all seriousness. "That's what he would need to do. Right, Mom?"

Two years after Shawn's death, I attended a COPS (Concerns of Police Survivors) retreat with eighty other widows of officers who have been killed in the line of duty. Out of everyone there, Suzie Sawyer, the executive director, had the most impact on me. She gave me a hug when I first arrived, and right away I knew I mattered.

One of our assignments that weekend was to traverse the high ropes course—a jungle gym of tightropes and beams twenty to fifty feet in the air. There were five sections to conquer, each presenting a different challenge. The theory behind it was that if we tackle our fears, whether real or invented, we will be able to overcome them and achieve our life goals.

I inhaled deeply and raised my hand to be the first volunteer. Someone put a harness around me and told me to climb the twenty feet to the first section of ropes. Once there, I was supposed to walk freehand across a twenty-foot log that was suspended at an incline. Although my harness was tied to a rope that went over a pulley and was held by one of the coaches, there was nothing to hang on to, so it felt as if I would fall.

Rigid with panic, I looked down at the ground far below. Every muscle in my body seized up. "Go for it, Jennifer!" Suzie hollered up at me. "Walk across. You can do it."

"I'm afraid I'll fall," I called back.

"You will not fall," she promised.

"What if I can't do this?" I argued, feeling ready to cry.

"You can do this, Jennifer," Suzie said, refusing to give up. "Think about it. Is this the hardest thing you have ever done?"

Breaths came out in bursts, and my face contorted, ready to cry. "No-o," I admitted.

"Is this your greatest pain, the biggest challenge you have ever faced?" she asked even louder.

Hot tears were starting to come. "No-o…"

"Is this your greatest fear?" Suzie asked. That woman was relentless!

My whole body was shaking. "No," I half whispered.

"You're right, Jennifer," Suzie continued. "The answer is *no*. You've already walked through your greatest fears, and, compared to that, this is nothing! So what are you afraid of? Let go of that beam and move!"

"But I didn't *choose* to have Shawn die and leave me all alone," I wailed to her and the others. "Why would I choose to place myself in this danger? I'm not strong enough to do this."

Then as I stood there, legs shaking, arms trying to balance myself, I sensed Shawn beside me. We were back in Honduras with the Peace Corps, crossing a river on foot because the bridge had been destroyed in a hurricane. Shawn instructed me, "When it's time to go, don't look back; just go. Let the momentum carry you forward, Jennifer. Now

23

move!" I hopped from stone to stone, afraid but moving ahead. If I hesitated, I knew that I would fall into the water.

To the group's delight, I let go of the beam, quickly crossed the log, and forged ahead to the second station where I was supposed to walk across a tightrope cable. I didn't pause very long for fear of losing my nerve, and I did *not* want to fail.

"Are you sure you have me?" I yelled to those below.

"We have you. You will not fall," Suzie and the others yelled, cheering over and over. "Look at you; you're doing it. Look at you!"

I made it across, and then, even though my hands were shaking violently, I had to switch safety locks to readjust my direction. With legs like noodles, I walked across two sideways planks and looked up. "Go up," Suzie hollered. "Don't stop; go up!"

"What's up there?" I yelled back.

"It's not important," Suzie countered, persistent and loud.

"I need to know what's ahead," I said.

"Take one step at a time and climb. Focus on what's in front of you. Deal with what is ahead when you get there." Suzie was demanding, but there was compassion in her voice.

Again I thought of Shawn and his persistent message to live "in the now." I scaled the pole and ascended to fifty feet above the ground. When I got there, I could see what Suzie had avoided telling me; two tightrope cords crossed at the center of the span forming a wide "X" that forced the climber's hands and feet to meet before they could cross to the other side.

This was impossible! There was no way my body could contort to those narrow parameters. Suzie and the others had stopped cheering and were frozen in silence. They watched closely, hoping I was up to the challenge. I plunged forward. I would have to figure it out as I went along. I forced myself to keep moving and somehow made it across. I had done what appeared to be impossible.

Now there was only one obstacle left: the Spider's Web—a net of ropes with an opening in the center. I stepped down into the woven design while the onlookers yelled at me to free-fall from fifty feet so the pulley system could lower me to the ground.

"It's mind over matter," Suzie yelled. "Let yourself fall forward. If you can do this one, you can do anything!" I took a big breath, held it, and fell forward. To my amazement, it was exhilarating—the best part of the whole ordeal.

"I did it! I did it!" I shouted, unhooking my harness and dropping to the ground. I sounded just like Maddi, who jumps up and down while shouting those same words.

Suzie gave me a huge hug, and the others followed suit. Relief mixed with pride, and I felt a new strength rise up within. Shawn was no longer with me, but with God's help I would find a new strength of my own. My family would take on a *new* normal. The children and I would be able to conquer whatever challenges came our way.

Guiding Principles

A Pinch of Salt

> Choose your fear and conquer it. Walk through your pain, and you will eventually see the other side. If you step out in faith, you will overcome the very thing that paralyzes you. If you don't, you can get stuck in your past and forfeit your future.

> Remember this: God designed us to overcome, and the God we cling to is our only strength. Surrender your fear of failing to Him, and let Him take you across your hurdles. It is not about failure; it's about trust. "So do not throw away your confidence; it will be richly

rewarded. You need to persevere so that when you have done the will of God, you will receive what he has promised" (Heb. 10:35–36).

> Be brave! Don't act in a boastful manner but in a God-fearing, God-trusting kind of way. God is carving out a path for you. Walk through the panic, dread, and apprehension, and you will arrive at a place where you can rejoice in trials overcome, spirits uplifted, and heartaches ultimately healed. "I have raised you up for this very purpose, that I might show you my power and that my name might be proclaimed in all the earth" (Exod. 9:16).

> Nurture and encourage your children. They are a precious gift from God. Teach them to respect and revere their parents, and if their father is deceased, help them understand the reality of eternal life in heaven for those who love Jesus.

> Three days before he died, Shawn read this passage aloud to me from the book *Captivating*: "Live when the pulse of life is strong. Life is a tenuous thing…fragile, fleeting. Don't wait for tomorrow. Be here now! Be here now! Be here now!"[1]

> Think of ways you can live the importance of today.

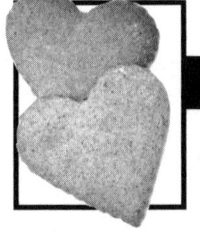

Homemade With Heart

One of Jennifer's Favorite Recipes

Jennifer likes to cook in big quantities and freeze meals for later use. She and Shawn would spend one whole weekend cooking, then freeze the food in meal-sized portions.

Chicken pot pie is Jennifer's favorite meal to serve to friends, not only because it is homemade, delicious, and nutritious, but also as a way of expressing her love. She makes enough filling for eighteen pies at one time. For a quick and easy meal, she removes one package of the filling and one package of piecrusts from the freezer, thaws them, assembles the pie, and bakes it. All quantities are for two pies unless otherwise specified.

Chicken Pot Pies

1 whole chicken
   (about 3 cups cooked; or use several chicken breasts) (for 18 pies, use 27 cups)
1 pkg. (10 oz.) frozen peas and carrots
   (for 18 pies, use 90 oz.) (you can also use green beans or corn)
1 pkg. (10 oz.) frozen cubed potatoes (optional)
   (for 18 pies, use 90 oz.)
½ cup onion, chopped
   (for 18 pies, use 4½ cups)
½ cup fresh mushrooms, chopped
   (for 18 pies, use 4½ cups)
¼ cup butter or margarine
   (for 18 pies, use 2¼ cups)
½ cup organic flour (for 18 pies, use 4 cups)
1½ cups water
   (for 18 pies, use 6 cups)
   (you may use the liquid poured off the chicken too)
¼ cup half-and-half (for 18 pies, use 2¼ cups)
¾ cup milk (for 18 pies, use 6¾ cups)
2 chicken bouillon cubes (for 18 pies, use 18 cubes)
½ tsp. salt (for 18 pies, use 4½ tsp.)
¼ tsp. sage (for 18 pies, use 2¼ tsp.)
⅛ tsp. pepper (for 18 pies, use 1⅛ tsp.)
¼ cup pimiento, chopped (for 18 pies, use 2¼ cups)
¼ cup snipped parsley (for 18 pies, use 2¼ cups)

Lawry's seasoned salt (optional; use to taste)
4 Pillsbury 9-inch piecrusts

Place a whole chicken (or several chicken breasts) in a kettle and add just enough water to cover. Bring to a boil, and then simmer about 15 minutes until the pink is gone. Drain the liquid and set aside. Cool the chicken, and then pull the meat off the bones in bite-sized pieces. Set aside for later use.

Cook frozen vegetables according to the package directions. Drain the liquid.

Cook the onion and mushrooms with the butter in a large skillet or kettle until tender but not brown. Quickly stir in the flour, then immediately add the water (or liquid from chicken), half-and-half, milk, bouillon cubes, salt, sage, and pepper.

Cook and stir until thickened and bubbly. Cook 1–2 minutes more, and then add the cooked chicken and vegetables, pimiento, parsley, and seasoned salt. Heat until bubbly. NOTE: The mixture should have the consistency of a casserole. Add more water if it looks too thick or more flour if it looks too thin.

Prepare each pie using one piecrust on the bottom and one on top. Flute the edges. Cut a few decorative slits in the top crust. Bake at 400°F for 30–45 minutes until golden brown.

Scoop the remaining filling into freezer bags in pie-sized portions. It takes approximately 3½ cups to make one pie. Keep extra pie crusts in the freezer for ready access.

Now for an Update

With a Cherry on Top

As a tribute to Officer Shawn Silvera, Jennifer and her friends established a Web site at www.shawnsilvera.com. Since the time of his death, Jennifer blogs several times a week, sharing her journey through grief as a way of helping others. (You can access her blog under the Journal tab.) She is also an advocate for the COPS organization. (Their Web site is www.nationalcops.org.)

Jennifer has a vibrant speaking ministry and is writing a book to encourage young mothers with the message that even in times of severe loss or pain, there is hope. Watch for her new book to be released soon.[2]

Two

Gather the Ingredients

BEING ON YOUR OWN CAN SEEM OVERWHELMING IF YOU are not prepared. It can feel like being pummeled by boxes tumbling from an overhead cabinet. We wonder how to make sense of the chaos. We need to find a system, a method, or a list of resources to tell us precisely how to begin.

For fifty years, Janet Leck's husband filled the gas tank, paid the bills, and made financial decisions. After his death, she faced not only recovery from grief but also the reality of unpaid bills, financial obligations, and new technology. Challenged by God to pare down her responsibilities, she was determined to "Simplify! Simplify! Simplify!"

After being controlled, managed, rejected, and abused for years, Elizabeth Turner wondered if she could stand on her own and still give her children a home. God taught her to say, "I refuse to lose," when He showed her His provision and love.

Shary VanDemark hoped she wasn't out of whatever it would take to blend the responsibilities of wage earner, mother, and student. "Sufficient Grace" finds Shary using innovation and creativity to make the best use of what she has on hand. In the process, she preserved a sense of family for her two little boys and fashioned a bit of beauty in her own life.

We can either muddle through our suffering with a trial-and-error approach, adding seasonings and tasting often, hoping to find the perfect formula—or we can turn to God and search His Word, relying on His recipe for our lives, using His ingredients, and drawing on His resources with a thankful heart.

Simplify! Simplify! Simplify!

A conversation with Janet Leck

And my God will meet all your needs according to his glorious riches in Christ Jesus.

—PHILIPPIANS 4:19

Now what?

I sat in the quiet of my condo, on the porch overlooking the nature preserve. All of creation lay before me. I needed a break because I had been floundering in a pile of bills to pay and tasks to do all morning. My petition for patience and guidance grew from my new station in life—on my own.

Talking to God was easy, and I trusted that He was listening. Still, He was not forthcoming with answers. Not right then. But later in the day, the wisdom of His Spirit seemed near. I heard one word: "Simplify!"

When I questioned what I had heard, the only response was: "Simplify! Simplify! Simplify!"

D'Arcy (pronounced *Darcy*) and I had been married for more than fifty years when he was diagnosed with prostate cancer. We prayed for healing and believed God would provide it through faith and medical treatment. So his doctors administered radiation therapy, and the tumor's progress slowed for a little while. But then the cancer crept into his bones. Throughout the ordeal, D'Arcy continued to lead a weekly Bible study for men at a nearby prison. He had served as the leader for nearly twenty-five years and hated the thought of giving it up.

Our prayers continued, but the cancer stepped up its relentless march. It wrapped itself around his spinal column until he couldn't walk. Soon he was dependent on a wheelchair and too tired to continue his ministry.

Then one day he could no longer get out of bed. After a period of time in the hospital, we arranged for hospice care so he could be at home. "You know," he said, "I think the healing the Lord has in mind for me is divine and eternal restoration. He is going to take this cancer-ridden body with all its limitations and let me trade it in for a vibrant, eternal body."

He said the words with great peace. I squeezed his hand and raised it to my lips.

Then he said, "The car needs an oil change."

The car needs an oil change? It seemed absurd. But D'Arcy's sense of responsibility had taken over. He was caring for me.

"Would you get something for me to write with, please?" he asked. Still numb from his oil change announcement, I walked down the hall and into our home office to grab a tablet and pen. I wondered why he wanted it. When I returned to the bedroom, he scooted himself up in bed and reached for the pen and paper. With barely enough strength to sit, he started a list.

I smoothed his rumpled hair and glanced at the pad as he wrote. Slowly and with great effort, he itemized the household bills. "These are the first ones you need to pay," he said, pointing.

I sat on the edge of the bed with the list in my hand and faced my own denial. These were the bills *I* needed to pay, meaning he would not be here. His stoic acceptance helped me face the truth. Now I *knew* he would die.

The writing exhausted D'Arcy, and he fell asleep. I slipped the pen from his fingers and covered his bare arm. Then I picked up my Bible and turned to a New Testament verse that had so often encouraged me during rough times: "I can do everything through him who gives me strength" (Phil. 4:13). I prayed:

> *Oh, Lord, please give me strength. Give me the love and grace*
> *I need to serve D'Arcy until he goes home to You.*

A few days later I told D'Arcy it was April 28. I wanted to see if the date held any significance for him. He smiled and whispered, "It's our fifty-first anniversary, isn't it?" I nodded and gave him a kiss.

Three days later, D'Arcy traded in his cancer-ridden body for a perfectly healed one that would serve him for eternity.

During those first difficult months after his death, I was so thankful for the times D'Arcy and I had spent together in God's Word. Two years before his death we had studied Revelation, the last book of the New Testament. One passage in particular brought me great comfort because it describes what Christians experience when they get to heaven.

> They are before the throne of God and serve him day and night in his temple; and he who sits on the throne will spread his tent over them. Never again will they hunger; never again will they thirst. The sun will not beat upon them, nor any scorching heat. For the Lamb at the center of the throne will be their shepherd; he will lead them to springs of living water. And God will wipe away every tear from their eyes.
> —REVELATION 7:15–17

I could picture D'Arcy in heaven near the throne of the Almighty—safe and joyous under God's protective tent. Our heavenly Father had provided for my husband, and now, in the early days after his death, I wondered how He would provide for me. That's when the prompting of the Holy Spirit took hold with one word: "Simplify!"

All through our marriage I had done what many women of my generation did: I let my husband take care of the tasks I thought were too complicated or time-consuming. I did not know how to change the oil in the car, for example, or even how to get someone else to do it. I needed to learn how to fill the gas tank and to understand the fine points of my car insurance. I wondered whom I would call if I was in an accident. Whom should I ask about the financial affairs?

The list was daunting and went on from there. I was suddenly mired in responsibilities that I felt ill-equipped to handle.

Again I thought about that prompting from the Holy Spirit. Simplify? I would love to do that, but how? Then a thought leaped into my mind—stop balancing the checkbook.

It was not that I didn't know *how* to reconcile my check register; it just never came out quite right. After hours of trying to balance my bank statement, I wanted to sweep my arm across the table and send everything flying! So I came up with a solution that worked for me. Instead of writing a check for each one of my expenses, I started using a credit card for the majority of my purchases. I am always very careful and disciplined to spend only what I know I can pay at the end of the month. Then I only need to write one check each month to pay off the credit card balance in full. It is much easier for me that way.

I also decided to set up three checking accounts from which I write only a few checks a year. One account is for tithing and charitable giving. One is for home and car insurance, the monthly credit card bill, and other large but infrequent expenses that I don't want to automatically pay via credit card. And the third checking account is for receiving dividend payments and paying my annual tax bills. Since I write only a few checks a year from each of these accounts, balancing them is a simple task.

To provide an extra layer of protection, my son-in-law said, "Let's go to the bank together. We'll sign you up for the Private Client Program."* That was a great comfort. God was my spiritual advocate. Now I had a financial advocate too.

Next, my children wanted me to get a cell phone, so I went to the mall and talked with a young man at the phone kiosk. He helped me pick one out and told me how to key in the names and numbers for my contact list. I thanked him and went to sit at a nearby bench. Every few minutes I went back and asked more questions and then returned to my bench. Back and forth I went until I had a list of names and numbers.

Proud of myself and feeling bolder, I went to the kiosk one more time and asked, "Now what about those Bluetooth things?"

"Oh," he said, with an exasperated wave of his arms. "That is *way* too complicated for you."

"Never mind," I said, knowing that *complicated* is not compatible with *simplify*.

While the emotional part of healing was not easy, I found it could be tailored to my needs. I had been active in prison ministry too, and as soon as I felt able, I joined a team of men and women who were leading a four-day Christian retreat at a local women's prison. Supporting and encouraging others was a great way to take the focus off myself. I also joined a grief group, and learned that grieving is an individual process. Talking and listening to others' stories was fine, but God helped me find different resources that were more helpful to me.

Mostly I relied on Scripture and a few other good books. I read a devotional called *Grieving the Loss of Someone You Love*.[1] One of the many issues it addressed was guilt—a plaguing guilt that said, "You

---

* Individual **Private Client Programs** are provided by some banks and investment service companies to offer their customers one-on-one investment and financial coaching.

should have looked for alternative cancer treatments. You should have done more to help D'Arcy." Slowly I learned not to blame myself anymore. Even my emotional clutter was simplified.

Near the end of the first year after D'Arcy died, I found another helpful resource called *The Widow's Workbook*.[2] This was the meat that got me through some of my toughest days. The study addressed all the issues I had stuffed away, and it got to the core of things I didn't even know I was ignoring. Clearly I was on the mend.

God didn't provide the kind of healing D'Arcy and I had originally prayed for, but He walked with us through the entire journey of D'Arcy's illness. The Lord is still caring for us on a daily basis—D'Arcy is safe under His heavenly tent, and I am secure under His earthly protection. Along the way I have learned that grieving and growing are not simple. But with God's help, they can be greatly simplified.

Guiding Principles

A Pinch of Salt

> Visualize your loved one in heaven, safe from the world's wickedness. "…and no one understands that the righteous are taken away to be spared from evil. Those who walk uprightly enter into peace; they find rest as they lie in death" (Isa. 57:1–2).

> Open the door of your heart to God, even if it's only a crack. When D'Arcy and I were first wed, we kept God on the fringe of our marriage instead of at the center of our lives. But little by little our focus changed, and by the time crisis hit, the Lord was our firm foundation, and we could not be shaken. What a comfort God's Word has been.

> Accept invitations that will simplify your life. I hate driving at night, so when friends call and ask, "Would you like a ride?" I love it and am relieved. They are always happy to pick me up if we are headed to the same place.

> Stand firm as an example to your children. Let them see your strength and hope so that someday when they face challenges, they will know how to cope. "But in your hearts set apart Christ as Lord. Always be prepared to give an answer to everyone who asks you to give the reason for the hope that you have" (1 Pet. 3:15).

Homemade With Heart

One of Janet's Favorite Recipes

D'Arcy loved meat loaf. This is a family favorite that I watched my mother make. She didn't have the recipe written anywhere, but I memorized it from watching her. I tweaked it over the years until I got it just right. I still enjoy it when I need a nice hot meal, and then I have plenty of leftovers for meat loaf sandwiches.

Janet's Meat Loaf

⅓ cup rolled oats
⅓ cup milk
⅓ cup ketchup
2 eggs, slightly beaten
2 tsp. seasoned salt
1 lb. meat loaf mix (consists of veal, pork, and beef)
1 lb. lean ground beef

Mix oats, milk, ketchup, eggs, and salt together in a bowl. Add the meats and knead with your hands until mixed.

Shape and place into a greased 4 x 8 inch loaf pan. Drizzle some ketchup on top. Bake for 1 hour at 350° F.

Now for an Update

With a Cherry on Top

Janet continues to volunteer in prison ministry by working on retreat weekends once or twice a year. She also participates in monthly prayer services with the inmates. With her newfound independence, Janet has no trouble making travel arrangements to visit her out-of-town children and grandchildren. She continues to be ever on the lookout for ways to keep life simplified.

I Refuse to Lose

A conversation with Elizabeth Turner

> I have loved you with an everlasting love; I have drawn you with loving-kindness. I will build you up again and you will be rebuilt.
>
> —JEREMIAH 31:3–4

My father didn't like me very much. And because my mother was aloof and a perfectionist, she liked me even less.

Dad, educated as a lawyer, chose his words carefully. He would aim them at a target and let fire with vocabulary intended to persuade, intimidate, control, or even destroy. My problem was that he practiced his sport on me. Whatever I said, he could think of a better way to express it: "You *should* have said..." he would reply, or "What you *meant* to say was..."

My father thoroughly enjoyed his relentless game. At other times he analyzed my personality. He thought that by consistently pointing out my faults, he could improve me. "Do you know why people don't like you?" he would ask. "It's because you're nervous." His description of me would go on from there, getting more specific.

Mother was even harder to please. She was the perfect wife back when wives were supposed to be perfect. Her friends adored her. She kept busy taking care of the house and left me alone unless I did something that disturbed her. I, being too creative and independent for her taste, never lived up to her expectations. Nothing I did suited her.

Surviving in that pain-filled household was like living in slow motion. I learned early on that keeping quiet was in my best interest. I was introverted anyway. In my imagination I created a future fantasy life, picturing a handsome prince who came to snatch me away on his powerful white horse.

My life was *managed* during the formative years, and then my adulthood was *prescribed*. I would go to college, become an elementary school teacher, and find a good husband.

It was at the university that I met James—handsome, smart, and certain to be a success. Daring, self-confident, and assertive, he was always having fun. "If only I could be more like him," I thought. He was my perfect escape. Even though he never told me he loved me, it seemed like love.

"You'd better grab him while you can," my parents said. "He's probably the best you're going to get." They both liked him—better, in fact, than they liked me. So I finished college, took a teaching position, and married James.

After longing for children for five years, we had three. Both James and I loved them, and I quit my full-time teaching job so I could stay at home. We took the children to church three times a week, and like little sponges, they soaked up the faith.

It wasn't very long before it became evident that James couldn't make enough money to support our family. He changed jobs often— either he couldn't get along with someone at work, he couldn't do what was required of him, or he just quit out of boredom. I did some substitute teaching, but permanent positions were impossible to find. We lived in apartments, but I longed for the day when we could have a nice house.

A few years later, I was able to buy a house with little money down and then trade it for a building lot under contract for deed. I had dreamt about designing my own home, and I let loose my creativity. Why can't we have a big, three-story house built into the side of the hill? How about a one-of-a-kind plan with rooms here and there, towers and skylights, and two-story windows to let in the light? The house plans were ambitious, but so was I. We had no money, but I believed it could happen. Everything would work out somehow.

Before we could start building, James quit his job again. Without my knowledge, he made arrangements for our family to move in with my father (my mother had died ten years before). I was devastated— once again forced to live under my father's condescension. Now he and James were on the same side, and both were verbally abusive.

We lived with my father for two and a half years, and every dollar we got was spent building the house. After a while I came to the real-ization that money or no money, I had to be free of my father.

At my insistence, we took the three children and moved into the new house. The interior walls were only two-by-four studs. Building mate-rials and moving boxes lay strewn across the plywood floors. I continued as a substitute teacher, and James worked part-time here and there. We lived in constant tension, but now that we were in our own home, I started standing up for myself when James got abusive. Whenever I did, though, his temper would explode like a stick of dynamite.

One night as I lay sleeping in our bed—a mattress on the plywood floor—James barreled into the room. He pulled off my covers, clutched them to himself, and yelled nonstop for an hour—then two, then three, and more. I lay there shivering in my nightgown, afraid to move, thinking, "The children can hear us; the children can hear us." When I finally tried to scramble out of bed, he grabbed my neck, held me against the wall, and continued to yell in my face. Once in a while he stopped to kick at boxes and throw things across the room. His tirade lasted all night. The next morning he taunted and bullied me, physically blocking every door I tried to go through.

For the first time in our twenty-three years of marriage, I started to think about divorce. I knew I would have to be strong and able to support my children. I drove to the university that very afternoon, applied for financial aid, and registered for graduate school.

At my insistence, James and I went to a Christian marriage counselor. After a few sessions, he called me in for a private consultation. He sat behind his desk frowning, and when he finally looked up, he said, "James has a serious personality disorder. The cause is physical, and it will not get better."

It was as if someone threw me over the side of a cliff and I was falling and falling. The nightmare I was living suddenly had a name as well as a prognosis. Emotions flooded my mind—shock, relief, fear, pity, sadness—each fighting for prominence. Things would have to change. *I* would have to change.

At a subsequent session, the counselor told him, "You're an abuser, James." Then he asked, "Isn't that right?" Instead of waiting for James to answer, the counselor turned to me and said, "If he does anything abusive to you again, you must call the police. Will you do that?"

I looked down at my hands trembling in my lap and nodded "Yes."

James yelled at me all the way home. But after that day in the counselor's office, the physical part of the abuse stopped.

I felt differently about our marriage after that. I secured a lawyer and told James to leave.

"I'm not leaving," he argued, and he continued to live with us for several more months. The number of arguments increased as I fought to hold my ground and didn't buckle as often to his demands.

Meanwhile, I prepared to assume sole responsibility for my family's financial needs. I applied for tuition grants and took graduate courses during evening and summer sessions. Within two years I had a master's degree, and a year after that, sixty additional credits. I took a full-time teaching position, worked in after-school programs with kids who were homebound or had behavioral problems, and taught summer school. Still, all I could afford was one carpenter for the house, but gradually the work progressed.

"Mommy, why are you always so tired?" the kids would ask. All I could do was try not to cry and be the best mother possible.

Later, James threatened to take half of the interest in the house. Since he couldn't give me anything for child support, I threatened right back and vowed to hire a lawyer if he didn't at least let the children and me have our home.

At the divorce hearing, I told the judge that James had a serious mental condition and that I would support the children. There was a forty-two-thousand-dollar lien—that James owed—on the property, so I took out a new mortgage to pay that off too.

With the divorce behind me, I took stock of my mental and emotional state. The cost had been high. My frazzled nerves made my skin so tender it felt raw. My girlfriend Roxanne took me under her wing and for five years listened to my problems and prayed. I was not angry with God (He brought me through years of abuse), but I did not think of Him as a warm and cozy father figure either. Roxanne reminded me that regardless of my feelings, God loved me. She prayed and prayed and prayed for me.

Something else that aided my healing was the book titled *Co-dependent No More: How to Stop Controlling Others and Start Caring for Yourself*.[3] I not only *felt* every word, but in a way, I also *was* every word. "I'm not going to be like that anymore," I told myself. "With God's help, I can change."

Gradually I came out of a life of anxiety and could think, learn, and function normally. Over time I was able to finish the house, and I enjoyed buying quality furnishings and artwork at bargain prices. I passed the admissions test and joined MENSA, an international organization that meets regularly for intellectual discussion. There I met new friends, and we talked about stimulating topics that didn't include any personal angst. On Wednesday nights I took art lessons.

My children are now grown, but I still live in that house. Each time I step into the foyer, I see a unique design, quality workmanship, beautiful furnishings, and fine art gracing the walls. Beauty and peace reside here, serving as a visible testimony to what happens when God smiles on your life.

Guiding Principles

A Pinch of Salt

- Keep on going, and do not stop. Persevere through every obstacle, and explore your options as you forge ahead. Work hard. Refuse to lose!

- Do not diminish yourself by saying, "I can't do this," or "I don't deserve anything good." Even though you may be at rock bottom, you are of great worth in God's eyes.

Trust Him even when you feel hopeless, and He *will* come to your aid.

> Work hard to break away from codependency. Tap into the many resources available and educate yourself. Decide to change, and resolve not to get caught in the same traps over and over. Make healthy choices, and stick to them.

> Do not underestimate what you can do with a small amount of money. When it comes to furnishing your home, look for markdowns, sales, coupon specials, and closeouts in stores that sell quality merchandise. With very little amount of funds, you can surround yourself with an artistically rich environment you consider tasteful and soothing.

> Believe in God even if you don't feel warm and cozy about Him all the time. Perhaps you are worried about necessities like food, shelter, or clothing, or you doubt that He loves you. Look back at ways He has shown His faithfulness to you in the past, and adopt the mind-set that He is going to do it again. The only way you can live in real freedom is with God's help.

Homemade With Heart

One of Elizabeth's Favorite Recipes

This flavorful pudding had its origins in Scandinavia, and based on what I've heard, my Swedish ancestors came through some tough times too.

Swedish Rice Pudding

1 cup uncooked white rice
2 cups water
5 cups milk
3 Tbsp. butter
½ cup sugar
Pinch of salt
4 eggs, beaten
6 Tbsp. cinnamon
1 cup raisins (optional)

Heat the rice and water in a covered four-quart saucepan.

When the mixture comes to a boil, reduce the heat to low and cook for 14 minutes. Add milk to the hot rice and simmer uncovered for about 45 minutes until slightly thickened. Stir occasionally to prevent burning.

Add in the butter, sugar, salt, and eggs (add the eggs slowly while stirring so they don't congeal).

Transfer the rice mixture to a greased, two-quart casserole or bowl. Stir in the cinnamon and raisins.

Set the bowl of rice into a pan of water about ½-inch deep. Bake at 350°F for 1½ hours until the top is brown and an inserted toothpick comes out clean. The top will be brown when done.

Serve either warm or cold with milk, cream, or whipped cream.

Now for an Update

With a Cherry on Top

Elizabeth persevered in her faith, dreams, and goals for several years as a single mother. Then one day she noticed a newspaper ad that read, "Looking for someone who's a Christian..." She sensed God prompting her to respond, and she met Darrian. They were married a year later, and they have celebrated many anniversaries since. They are both gourmet cooks and especially enjoy making magnificent desserts. Every day Darrian makes it a point to express his love.

Elizabeth is now retired from teaching and is busy pursuing a variety of interests. She is active in her church and is an accomplished artist who exhibits her work through the local art society.

Sufficient Grace

A conversation with Shary VanDemark

> For the material they had was sufficient and more than enough for all the work, to perform it.
> —EXODUS 36:7, NASU

There! I placed a droplet of glue on the bottom of a teeny vase of flowers. Then I anchored the little arrangement to a miniature tabletop. Voila! My dream-come-true floral shop was complete.

I stepped back to admire the quaint little building with its checkered tile floor strewn with leaves, stems, and blossoms. I loved the sign in the window that said "VanDemark Designs" and the bell on the door that rang with a tiny ding. Coolers and counters were lined with floral arrangements in a multitude of sizes and colors. I could almost smell the sweetness in the air. The prototype was complete. If only life could be as pleasant and sweet as that little shop.

I remember when my marriage began to disintegrate. I felt so alone and sad. I thought I had been fulfilling my role as a wife, mother, and homemaker exactly the way I was supposed to. I believed in God, but I wondered, "Why did this happen, Lord? Have I asked too much from life?"

My dreams had been in full bloom, and I wanted to do all the right things to keep them growing. I consistently tried to save our marriage, but it just didn't work out. I watched helplessly as it slowly wilted, and then it died.

"The boys and you are a ball and chain around my neck," my husband had said. Finally, I got the message. So I agreed with the terms of the divorce and felt grateful for the family we had created.

"Let go, and let God," my well-meaning friends reminded me, quoting the popular saying. It was a great piece of advice, but in the meantime, I knew I did not dare give up. Even though I felt rejected and wanted to wallow in self-pity, there were urgent matters at hand. I went from being part of a couple to being a struggling-to-survive breadwinner. Suddenly I faced decisions that would impact how my little boys and I would fare.

Whom can I rely on? Will I be able to afford day care? How can I earn an income? These were questions that needed answers. It was all so overwhelming.

My cute-as-bugs little boys were just six and three, and I wanted to be at home with them as much as possible. I took a part-time job as a checkout clerk at the local grocery store and also sold cosmetics door-to-door. That generated barely enough income for groceries and incidentals. If I was going to earn a meaningful wage, I needed to find affordable day care, especially for Matthew, who was not yet in school.

I knew I needed to rely on *Someone* other than myself. One night when I flopped into bed, exhausted and discouraged, I cried out, "Lord, what am I going to do?"

"I'm here," God seemed to say. "Talk to Me. Pour out your troubles. Tell Me your needs." I pounded my pillow and talked to God a lot that night—sometimes not very nicely. But He was able to take it, and my ranting calmed me down. I settled into a peaceful sleep and woke up refreshed the next morning. But I was still without clear direction on how to plan the next stage of my life.

That evening I went to church—a large congregation a few blocks from my home—where I taught religious education classes to grade-school kids. At the end of the evening, I pulled out of the parking lot and noticed Sister Lucy, one of our nuns, heading back to her house. I wanted to talk with her, but it was getting late. "Maybe tomorrow," I thought.

The next afternoon I gave Sister a call and explained my newly divorced status.

"I just don't know what to do," I said. "Michael, my six-year-old, is in kindergarten, but I also have Matthew, who is only three. Who can I trust to take care of him?"

"I know someone who wants to do day care," she said. "Her name is Katherine; she has a little guy too, and she is looking for a playmate for him. Katherine is very kind and would provide loving care for Matthew. Maybe that would free you up to work a few more hours." I wrote the woman's name and phone number on a scrap of paper.

Meanwhile, the boys poked and jabbed at each other and circled around me, as they often did when I was on the phone. "Thank you, Sister," I said, my heart a little lighter with her concern for me. I hung up the phone and said, "C'mon, boys. Let's have some grub." We were becoming a team—just the three of us.

The next day I called Katherine. Someone answered on the second ring, and I heard the voice of a pleasant-sounding woman. "Hello, this is Katherine," she said, and I could almost see her smile.

I told her who I was, and she replied, "Yes, Sister Lucy told me you might call. Would you and your little boy like to stop over this afternoon?" I accepted her invitation.

The minute she opened the door and I saw her little boy standing beside her, I felt at ease. She bent down to talk with Matthew, and soon the two boys were off to play.

Katherine and I visited awhile and discovered we had many things in common. She became a trusted and caring friend I could count on, often listening to my anxious insecurities. Most importantly, Matthew loved her and became best friends with her son. Sometimes she didn't even charge me for taking care of him. I had a suspicion that Sister Lucy *knew* that Katherine and I would become good friends.

Others at my church looked out for me too. Ours was a stewardship church dedicated to taking care of its own parishioners as well as reaching out to others. At Thanksgiving, one of the members came to my door and said, "Shary, we know you have a lot of pride, but please accept this offer." With that he handed me a large basket filled with all the fixings for a Thanksgiving dinner.

If I was going to survive financially, I knew it would take more than help from good friends and my church. Daily I poured out my woes to God. I listened with my heart for His guidance, and He seemed to urge me to take stock of my talents, my abilities, and what I liked to do.

"Lord, I don't have impressive degrees that can help me to earn a big income," I told Him again and again. But God didn't seem to care about what I *didn't* have. I got the sense He wanted me to focus on what I *did* have. Although I was busy with the boys and the humdrum responsibilities of keeping the household running, I knew I had a creative side too. "I really like flowers," I told the Lord. "Could I earn a living doing something I love?"

I was excited, almost giddy. I dug out the phone book and started my research. I scanned page after page until I found a technical college less than a half hour away. It had just the classes I needed, so I enrolled and learned the fine points of floral design—along with how to juggle work, school, and caring for two rambunctious boys.

I was tired most of the time, but soon I had a degree in a field I loved. I learned as much as I could about marketing too. All that knowledge served me well when I began working for floral shops and design studios around town.

Eventually I turned a room downstairs into a cute little place where I could create fresh or silk flower arrangements. That way I could work out of my home on weekends and keep an eye on my sons. Ever on the lookout for opportunity, I was excited when I discovered even more ways to boost my income. I taught flower arranging on a cable television show, and I also taught community education classes in the local school district.

With God's help I have grown from a scared young woman to an independent business owner. The journey has not been easy, and it is not over yet. Meanwhile, I still have my miniature floral shop—not the life-sized one yet—and I am looking forward to what lies ahead as I continue to listen to God and focus on what I *can* do.

Guiding Principles

A Pinch of Salt

> ➤ Believe there is something better ahead no matter how old you are. Have hope. Try not to worry. "And why are you worried...? Observe how the lilies of the field grow; they do not toil nor do they spin, yet I say to you that

not even Solomon in all his glory clothed himself like one of these" (Matt. 6:28–29, NASU).

> ➤ Create something—work with miniatures. Try your hand at painting, ceramics, knitting a scarf, or writing a poem. We all need ways to escape the cares of the world.

> ➤ Focus on God. Even if your expectations for other people are reasonable, those individuals might not be there for you. But you can always count on God's strength within you.

> ➤ Make a list of your talents and resources. Try to match your income-earning ability with something you love to do.

> ➤ The Lord never promised us a life without pain. He only promised that He would be there for us. But remember, He can't help us if we don't let Him in.

Homemade With Heart

One of Shary's Favorite Recipes

When the boys were little and money had to be budgeted carefully, a good pot of chicken stew warmed up our home. My grandma always had Bisquick on hand, and it became a staple in my kitchen too. Chicken and dumplings often came to the rescue when the boys and I needed a good dose of comfort food.

Chicken and Dumplings

1 whole chicken
1 or 2 cans no-fat chicken broth
2 cups each carrots and celery, chopped

1 cup onion, chopped
1 tsp. salt (optional—I serve unsalted)
1 to 1½ cups flour
Cold water
Original Bisquick mix (enough for 12 biscuits)

Wash chicken and put into a six- to eight-quart pot; add just enough water to cover the chicken. Boil chicken until tender, then remove it from the pot. Cool the chicken and broth, and then chop or tear chicken into pieces, throwing away the skin and bones. Set chicken aside for later.

Skim fat from the top of the broth and discard. Add to the broth: canned chicken broth, carrots and celery, onion, and salt. Bring to a boil, then turn down the heat and simmer until the vegetables are tender.

In a small shaker or jar with a tight-fitting lid, combine and shake flour and cold water, adjusting the amounts of flour and water until it makes a thick cream. Slowly pour the cream mixture into the simmering broth, stirring until there are no lumps.

Make a batch of Original Bisquick mix according to directions on the box. Drop spoonfuls into the thickened broth, cover and cook 10 minutes, then uncover and cook 10 minutes more. The dumplings will have a cakelike texture when done.

Add the chicken pieces back in. Sprinkle the soup with garlic powder and parsley.

Serve with love.

Now for an Update

With a Cherry on Top

Shary is grateful for God's blessings and very real presence in her life. She is pleased that her boys have grown up to follow their own dreams. Michael is a writer working diligently on his career, and Matthew is a nurse at a large metropolitan hospital.

When Shary's not creating floral arrangements for weddings, graduations, and home and office décor, she still works with flowers. One of her favorite outlets is competing in the annual flower competition at the city art museum. She also takes great joy in creating arrangements to give away at local nursing homes, looking for just the people who need a little extra bloom in their lives. Shary is content and at peace. Every day, she gets closer to achieving her goal of opening her own floral design studio.

Three

Glaze With Hope

GLAZING MEANS ADDING LUSTER AND FLAVOR TO A FOOD by basting it as you heat it in the oven. To glaze a ham, for example, we can spread a syrupy mixture of brown sugar and spices over the top, adding a delicious shiny coat to the meat as it bakes. When a grieving woman showers her predicaments with prayer, she glazes her problems with hope. That is why a spiritual radiance is evident even as she struggles to ward off worry and develop a heightened trust in God.

Sandra Aldrich was left with two children to raise, and in "Milestone for a Single Mom" she voices some of her frustrations and disappointments. With the help of a few unsettling events—an unkind remark from a teacher, a light bulb that needed changing, and even a large black horse that would not cooperate—she learned to take her concerns to God.

Decision making can overwhelm someone who is newly single—especially when the status from married to solo is a sudden change. Thankfully, Judy Sieps knew where to put her hope. In "The Plans I Have for You," see how she took comfort from God's promise in Jeremiah 29:11 and put it to work in her life.

Lastly, read about Joanna Price, a quiet and shy twenty-two-year-old who, after a year of marriage, found herself divorced and in debt. Youthful wisdom told her that God was her only hope. "Jesus Is My

Bridegroom" is an account of how she established a career, worked her way into solvency, and stepped out in faith to serve God overseas.

Glazing with hope does not mean slathering your problems with camouflage and pretending that nothing is wrong. It means saturating your grief with prayer and discovering that when we put our hope and trust in God, the result is striking, flavorful, and lustrous.

Milestone for a Single Mom

A conversation with Sandra Picklesimer Aldrich

> For your Maker is your husband—the LORD Almighty is his name—the Holy One of Israel is your Redeemer; he is called the God of all the earth.
>
> —ISAIAH 54:5

My daughter, Holly, was in third grade when she came home one day in tears. The room mother had handed out directions to an event and said, "Take these home to your families."

Then she glanced at Holly and said, "Sorry. I mean, to your moms."

In our kitchen, I put my arm around my sobbing eight-year-old. "Holly, we are still a family, even though your daddy died," I said. "We are just a family of three now."

As she leaned against me in relief, I realized that if we were going to survive, I had to develop emotional strength. So I took a deep breath and leaned on the Scripture verse I found: "I can do everything through him who gives me strength" (Phil. 4:13).

Single moms (and single dads) need personal strength no matter how we gained our status. We all have too much stress, too many responsibilities, and too little time. In my own situation, I had married young and gone from my father's authority to my husband's authority. And even though I taught in a Detroit-area high school, handling numerous professional duties, I knew nothing about balancing the checkbook, doing home maintenance, or repairing a car. Those had been my husband's duties.

I also claimed Isaiah 54:5: "For your Maker is your husband—the LORD Almighty is his name." I drew special comfort from that verse since I was afraid of making decisions by myself, terrified that a wrong choice would jeopardize my children's future. So I prayed about everything—large and small. Amazingly, not only did I get direction, but also I learned it was OK to argue with the Lord a little bit!

For example, one morning I noticed the recessed light in the family room ceiling was out. It was time to drag out the tall ladder and change the light bulb. Perched on a narrow step, I started griping to God. His shoulders are pretty big, and He knows what we are thinking anyway, so I figured He could handle it. Besides, in Matthew 19:14, when Jesus said, "Come to me," He did *not* add, "But come with a smile on your face," or even, "Come without tears." He just said, "Come."

So I told my Husband, God of the universe, that *husbands* are supposed to change light bulbs and I should not have to do this. From there my complaining quickly escalated to thinking, "I should not have to be doing this single-parenting thing either."

When I was finished griping, I had the good sense to be quiet and listen. In that moment, it was just as though He said, "Try turning it the other way."

Try turning it the other way? But I know the light bulb–changing rule that says, "Righty tighty; lefty loosey." But my way wasn't working, so I gave that old bulb a halfhearted turn the other way—and it fell right into my hand!

Then it dawned on me; I saw how the bulb threads had been stripped and the previous light changer had forced the bulb into place, and I realized that God knew those threads were stripped, just as He knows the areas of my life where I am the weakest. So I determined to listen to Him more and trust all areas of daily life to my celestial Husband.

Next, I began to ponder how Philippians 4:19 applied. That was the verse my ten-year-old son, Jay, had been memorizing for Sunday school the day I came home from the hospital to tell him and his sister their dad had died. As I came through the back door that day, the typed verse sat on the kitchen counter and seemed to glow with special encouragement: "But my God shall supply all your need according to his riches in glory by Christ Jesus" (KJV).

I cling to that promise the way a drowning person clings to a life preserver. Occasionally I have even challenged my heavenly Father by asking, "Even *this* need, God?"

I was still learning that He doesn't overlook anything. As I continued to pray about every challenge and decision, He answered. Sometimes He used friends to show me how to change the oil in the car or to balance the checkbook. Other times He encouraged me through a glorious sunset and with the constant thought that He had not left me alone.

But most of all He helped me grow while I was helping my children grow.

Yes, I worried about raising my two children to be healthy adults. I wondered how I could teach Jay to be a man. So I kept our family in church, trusting those few hours each week to provide positive role models. Now, all these years later, Jay is a well-grounded, masculine young man, despite having grown up with a mother, a sister, and a neutered cat!

Still, in the midst of my gratitude, I remember many days when discouragement was a close companion. For example, one Saturday morning nothing seemed to go right. In the middle of my grumpiness, Holly—then in college—arrived home and insisted we go horseback riding.

"I might as well," I muttered. Within the hour, we were at our favorite stable, but the docile, brown horse I usually rode was already on the trail for the day. That gentle horse had two speeds—slow and stop—so I was disappointed that he wasn't available. There was nothing to do but request the second most docile ride.

Soon a large black horse was brought out. We eyed each other before I took the reins and led him to the mounting block. Once there, I placed my left foot in the stirrup and started to swing my right leg over the saddle just as the horse decided that he did not want me on his back. As he sidestepped away from the block, there I was—one foot in the stirrup and the other poised in midair.

Even back then, I did not have the agility to quickly shift my weight and throw myself into the saddle. The stable owner danced back and forth below me, his arms in the air as though to catch me when I fell. There was only one convenient part of my anatomy to push, but he knew me well enough to know that he had better not touch *that*.

So with arms waving, he hopped from foot to foot and yelled, "Don't quit *now*, ma'am! Don't quit now!"

Holly bent forward in her own saddle, howling with laughter, so I started chuckling and then had an even tougher time hauling myself into position. But finally, with a surge of adrenaline, I shifted my weight and shoved my right foot over and into the stirrup. The horse gave a defeated snort as I turned his head and followed a still laughing Holly up the trail.

That ride, even with its tenuous start, became a reminder to provide an extra push on tough days. No matter how tough my challenges are as a single mother, I don't dare quit—now or ever.[1]

Guiding Principles

A Pinch of Salt

- › Draw encouragement and strength from Scripture.

- › Remember, when you let go of worry, God's answers come into focus.

- › Claim Isaiah 54:5—God Himself provides like a husband.

- › Analyze and adjust. Be open to change, including adding some new family traditions.

- › Avoid the disappointment of expecting others to take on your hurt or fully understand your responsibilities.

- › Let yourself laugh again. "A cheerful heart is good medicine" (Prov. 17:22).

- › Do not quit! Give that extra push.

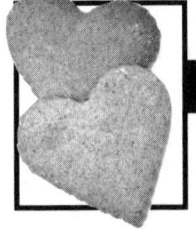

Homemade With Heart

One of Sandra's Favorite Recipes

If you have the time and the inclination, this made-from-scratch brownie recipe is delicious and features a hidden layer of green peppermint frosting.

Delectable Peppermint Brownies

½ cup water
½ cup butter or margarine plus 6 Tbsp. butter (3 Tbsp. softened)
4 Tbsp. cocoa
1 cup sugar
1¼ cups flour
1 tsp. baking soda
¼ cup milk plus 1½ Tbsp. milk
1 egg
⅛ tsp. salt
½ cup chopped walnuts (optional)
1½ cups powdered sugar
½ tsp. peppermint extract
2 drops green food coloring
¾ cup chocolate chips

Layer 1: Brownies

Put water, ½ cup butter or margarine, and cocoa into a kettle and bring it to a boil. Remove from heat, and mix in sugar, flour, and baking soda. Add ¼ cup milk, egg, and salt. Stir in walnuts.

Pour into a 9 x 9 inch greased pan and bake at 350°F for 30 minutes.

Layer 2: Green Peppermint Frosting

Combine powdered sugar, 1½ Tbsp. milk, and 3 Tbsp. softened butter. Stir in peppermint extract and green food coloring.

Spread evenly over the brownies while they are still warm. Chill thoroughly.

Layer 3: Chocolate Topping

Melt chocolate chips and remaining 3 Tbsp. butter. Stir until smooth.

Carefully spread the melted chocolate over the brownies, hiding the green frosting. Cool thoroughly.

Now for an Update

With a Cherry on Top

Sandra is the author or coauthor of seventeen books, and she is a well-known speaker who has appeared on such radio and television programs as *Focus on the Family*, *The 700 Club*, *Prime Time America*, and many more. Her speaking venues cover a wide range from Women of Virtue Conferences, women's and couple's retreats, college conferences, hospice seminars, and single-parent events to business meetings and military bases. She always presents the serious issues of life with insight and humor. Sandra's two children are now grown, and she makes her home in Colorado. She can be contacted through e-mail at BoldWords@aol.com.

The Plans I Have for You

A conversation with Judy Sieps

> "For I know the plans I have for you," declares the LORD, "plans to prosper you and not to harm you, plans to give you hope and a future."
>
> —JEREMIAH 29:11

I buttoned my coat and tied my scarf as I left the hospital and walked to the parking lot. The evening was bright and crisp, and moonlight reflected off the snow. It was the Christmas season. Hope and music filled the air.

But I was preoccupied, and my mind was lost in the events of the past few weeks. I talked to God as I drove the twenty miles back to the neighborhood where Wayne and I had raised our daughters, Diona, Rachel, and Colleen. I parked the car and walked into the house, which in Wayne's absence took on a dark and somber feel. As the door clicked shut behind me, a devastating thought crashed into my mind: "He is never coming home!"

I pushed the feeling away, but it came back. I wanted to wave my hand and make the thought disappear, but it settled around my heart like a mist, as if God were gently preparing me for an uncertain future. I sat on the couch and pressed my face into my hands. I knew that from now on, I would always walk through the door without Wayne.

After a painful struggle, my husband of thirty-two years went home to the Lord. Our daughters and I were at his bedside, trying to grasp the loss of a father and companion. He had been diagnosed with adrenal cancer only seven days before and had surgery in an attempt to remove the large mass. Everything had happened so fast. Sure, Wayne had a few health issues during the past few weeks, but we did not think he was going to die. He was only fifty-eight. "Lord, how can my soul mate be gone?" I cried.

Wayne had been a dependable partner and a comfortable companion. He loved to read, watch the news, and keep up with current events. If there was something I wondered about, I would go ask him. I always thought, "Wayne will know."

When I spent leisure hours puttering in my flower garden, he was nearby in his workshop in a corner of the garage. His shop was filled with hammers and nails, saws and screws, routers and wrenches. It was comforting just to hear him pounding and buzzing away, exhilarated at the prospect of creating something new.

But now he was gone. "How can I let go, Lord?" I asked. "What do I know about being alone?" So many decisions lay ahead, and I needed to make some plans.

Family and friends had gathered to help me through the funeral. In the weeks and months that followed, they often called to check on me or to invite me out to dinner or a play. But eventually, when it was time to make my way in the world as a single woman, I joined a *new* church congregation that had many resources for widows. I relied on their support groups and God's Word for comfort and guidance.

I browsed through bookstore shelves until I found a little devotional called *Making His Heart Glad*.[2] I found that little book with its daily stories and Scripture verses extremely helpful. I still use it from time to time.

But one day when I came home from work, I felt completely overwhelmed with this new life I was supposed to fit into. I set a pot of water on the stove and took a tea bag out of the cupboard. I settled onto the couch, picked up my Bible, and turned to the Old Testament, where I read, "'For I know the plans I have for you,' declares the LORD, 'plans to prosper you and not to harm you, plans to give you hope and a future'" (Jer. 29:11).

That was the kind of hope I needed! My future was filled with questions. Should I sell the house and move to Wayne's hometown in South Dakota as he and I had planned? Or should I move to Colorado where all three of our daughters live? How long should I keep his clothes? When should I sell his little blue Reatta convertible and his red truck? What should I do with all his tools? It didn't matter if a decision was big and complicated, or small and simple. It was still another decision that had to be made.

The teapot whistled, and I steeped a strong cup of tea. I let my weary mind slip into reflections of innocent days long ago. I smiled at the stir Wayne had caused in my small and conservative hometown shortly after I met him. I had only known him for a few months when he bought me an expensive birthday present—a Honda 90 motorcycle. He loved the outdoors and thought it would be fun for the two of us to ride our bikes and explore the surrounding plains and foothills together.

But my parents had a far different idea. "Nice girls do not ride around with young men on motorcycles," they said. I tried to explain that Wayne was trustworthy and that his intentions were honorable, but my protests did little good. I wondered how to break the news to Wayne. When he knocked at the front door the next day, I suggested we go for a walk.

"I'm sorry," I told him. "I'm not going to be able to share your love of adventure on a motorcycle. My parents will not allow me to go riding with you." Immediately I saw the disappointment in his eyes.

"I'm really sorry too," he replied. "I wasn't thinking. I didn't want to make a bad impression. I want your family to like me." The sincerity of his response touched my heart. I squeezed his hand and gave him a hug.

"Don't worry about it," I said. "It will all work out." As I had hoped, it didn't take long until his genuine interest in others and his easy-going personality took hold of my father and mother and everyone else in town. They soon saw the good-hearted person that he was.

I had not been focused on finding a man with lots of money, but the generosity of that first gift, and others after it, led me to believe that Wayne must be extremely wealthy. Soon I realized that was not the case. He had been raised on a farm and brought a set of practical values with him. He was generous, but not foolhardy; he was frugal, but not stingy. I admired that. And soon, with family and small-town friends supporting us, Wayne and I were married at the little church my parents attended.

Our marriage started on a positive note that remained steady throughout our years together. I felt secure in knowing Wayne was reliable and dependable and that he was a good worker as well. Our combined income provided a comfortable living, and we never spent more than we earned. Wayne worked as a journeyman press operator, and I became a nurse. We saved until we could buy a house that included a yard with room for a garden and a place for three little girls to play. We usually managed to have enough money for occasional dinners out and annual family vacations.

Though it seemed to be a long time away, we looked forward to growing old together. Wayne believed in having a plan for that too. He insisted on having a life insurance policy, and we consistently put money aside for retirement. We did not have large amounts to invest, but we were disciplined enough to save small amounts on a regular basis. When we visited our financial adviser, I often rolled my eyes with all the talk about stocks and bonds, mutual funds and money markets, and variable annuities and fixed annuities, but I tried to pay attention.

Later on I was grateful I had accompanied Wayne on those financial planning appointments. Those visits enabled me to know and trust the person who would guide me in creating a *new* plan—a plan for a single woman.

The phone rang and brought me back to the moment. My daughter Colleen was coming over with her friends, Julie and Stephan. Soon the house was filled with chatter and life, and my spirits were buoyed.

During our conversation, Stephan mentioned he was a law student who worked part-time in a legal office, and I was struck with an idea. "You are about the same size as Wayne, aren't you?" I observed as I sized him up. "Would you like to have some of his suits and ties?"

With a little urging, I got him to accept my offer. After a few minutes of trying clothes on in the bedroom, Stephan came out wearing a suit that fit him perfectly. I nodded and smiled, unable to speak at seeing vibrant life inside Wayne's clothes. But Stephan looked great, and I sent him home with several combinations of shirts, suits, and ties. He was pleased, and so was I. One of my little problems had been solved, and I had helped someone else at the same time. That felt good.

Eventually I saw God's hand in solving other problems too. At church I told the leader of my Grief Share group that I was struggling with my decision to sell the house. I told her about the opportunity to move to Wayne's hometown, or the possibility of settling in Colorado, where my daughters lived. She had experience and training in her ministry, and I trusted her.

"Don't do it," she advised. "Stay in your home for three to five years. This should not be a decision you rush into." I followed her advice, and I'm glad I did. Years later the house Wayne and I enjoyed together still provides a measure of comfort I don't think I would have found if I had moved. Another not-so-little problem had been solved.

My son-in-law Joel came to town one day and went into Wayne's workshop. He found several little red toolboxes Wayne had ordered through rebate offers. Joel selected a small hammer, pliers, a few wrenches and screwdrivers, and a variety of nails and screws to fill the boxes. He put one together for each of my daughters and one for me too. Joel's thoughtfulness gave the girls and me something that was an intimate part of Wayne's life.

I thought again about God's plans for us. It seemed that no problem or decision was too big or too small for God to care about as long as I trusted in Him and kept my heart open to the people He sent into my life.

This Scripture verse came to my mind: "I know the plans I have for you.... Then you will call upon me and come and pray to me, and I will listen to you. You will seek me and find me when you seek me with all your heart" (Jer. 29:11–13).

All those decisions and plans that needed to be made served a great purpose. They brought a wonderful variety of people into my life and provided opportunities for me to reach out to others. Most importantly, they kept me dependent on God for the true peace and comfort only He can give.

Guiding Principles

A Pinch of Salt

> Find a Scripture verse that consoles you, and claim it as your own. An Old Testament verse I relied on was, "The LORD is my strength and my song; he has become my salvation" (Ps. 118:14). I did not always feel like singing, but God often spoke to me and offered comfort through music.

> Look to God's Word for guidance. "You hold me by my right hand. You guide me with your counsel, and afterward you will take me into glory. Whom have I in heaven but you?" (Ps. 73:23–25).

> Rely on God. Nothing is too trivial to take to Him in prayer. He cares about everything that concerns you—even the number of hairs on your head. "Are not five sparrows sold for two pennies? Yet not one of them is forgotten by God. Indeed, the very hairs of your head are all numbered. Don't be afraid; you are worth more than many sparrows" (Luke 12:6–7). Take all of your problems to God, and don't rush into making big decisions.

> Understand that it's OK to feel sad. In some cultures people wear different clothes when they mourn. But in the West, we give no outward sign that we are grieving. It's all right to tell others about your sorrow or to let them see you cry. Do not shut them out. Give them an opportunity to show their love for you.

> Give yourself time to adjust to changes in your life. Do not expect to "get over" your loss in a few months or even a full year. Confide in those who have gone

through grief before you, and seek out well-trained professionals for help.

Homemade With Heart

One of Judy's Favorite Recipes

Wayne loved my banana cream pie so much that I was lucky to get even one piece when we had it in the house. If a friend came over and saw the pie sitting on the counter, Wayne would try to dissuade their enthusiasm by saying, "Oh, you don't want any of that. It has worms in it."

Banana Cream Pie

1 cup sugar
4 Tbsp. cornstarch
4 egg yolks, slightly beaten
2 cups milk
2 tsp. vanilla
2 Tbsp. butter
1 deep, 9-inch piecrust
2–3 bananas

Blend sugar and cornstarch. Add mixture to slightly beaten egg yolks. Then gradually add milk. Cook over medium heat, stirring frequently, until it comes to a rolling boil and thickens.

Remove from heat and add vanilla and butter. Pour half of the filling into a deep, 9-inch piecrust that has been baked and cooled. Add a layer of banana slices. Next, add remaining filling. Top with more banana slices.

Meringue Topping

4 egg whites
Dash of cream of tartar
4 Tbsp. sugar

Beat egg whites with an electric mixer until stiff peaks form. Add a dash of cream of tartar. Gradually add sugar and beat until sugar dissolves.

Spread the meringue over the top of pie to form decorative swirls, peaks, and valleys. Bake in a preheated 400°F oven for about 8 minutes or until browned. Cool thoroughly.

Now for an Update

With a Cherry on Top

After Judy's first year on her own, she gratefully accepted an invitation from her church to tell others at a widow's tea about God's guidance in reentering the single life. Since she and Wayne planned ahead and saved money for retirement, Judy doesn't need to work to support herself, but she found that she enjoys the camaraderie of having a full-time job. She continues to meet with her financial adviser on a regular basis—at least once or twice a year. Although she mourns the loss of their dreams for "growing old together," she is happy to have had thirty-two years with Wayne, and she continues to live in the house they shared. She makes frequent trips to visit her three daughters, two grandchildren, and son-in-law in Colorado.

Jesus Is My Bridegroom

A conversation with Joanna Price

The righteous cry out, and the LORD hears them; he delivers them from all their troubles. The LORD is close to the brokenhearted and saves those who are crushed in spirit.

—PSALM 34:17–18

Forests, canyons, creeks, and trails swoosh beneath me as I zip along the cable over mountainous terrain. Harnessed and helmeted, I dangle from the hoist and feel my adrenaline surge. *Whee!* The only thing I hear is the cable singing over my head, and I am not nearly as frightened as I was at first. "Thank You, Lord," my spirit shouts. "Your creation is awesome, and because of You, I am free!"

Five girlfriends and I are trying a new sport called zip-lining. I approach the platform in the giant ponderosa pine and hear them hooting and cheering my bravado. At this moment I love them all—Darlene, Cordelia, Ann, LeAnn, and Maggie—and Katie too, who is at home with her new baby. My friends mean the world to me.

Back home that evening, my dog, Molly, gives me that pitiful look that says she wants to sit with me on the couch. Part beagle, part springer spaniel, she was my dog of choice at the animal shelter last year. "OK, come on, then," I tell her, "but just this once. I had so much fun today, and I'm too tired to tell you no."

My life has not always been so happy and settled. About ten years ago I was married for only a year. I was in my early twenties, and in many ways I thought my life was over.

I met my future husband, Ted, at a picnic. Even though I was initially cautious, he pursued me with passion. He did everything with such aplomb—almost as if he had taken lessons on *how to catch the girl*. I will admit that I liked it. What nineteen-year-old wouldn't?

To prepare for our life together, we took a premarital counseling course at the church, but as our wedding day approached, I wondered if we were moving ahead too fast. Sometimes I would think, "Everyone gets cold feet, don't they? I'm probably just imagining things." So after dating for a year and a half, we headed for the altar.

We got our own apartment, and before long, I realized that Ted was ignoring me. It was like *the chase* was over. Our marriage was *in the bag*, and now he could pursue other interests. Because he was bored with me, he angered easily. Well, hey! I was angry too.

"Why did you buy that leather jacket?" I asked him one night when I spotted him wearing it. "You already have two."

"I don't need you telling me what I can and cannot buy," he shouted, looking mean. "Do you think I didn't notice the new coat you got last week?"

I suppose you could call it revenge spending. He would buy something, so I would go out and get something I wanted too. It didn't matter that we didn't have the money for it.

Our fights became more frequent and severe, and so did our spending. Our emotions were as supercharged as two little kids playing "king of the hill." Within months we had maxed out our credit cards.

Still, I *did* want to work on our marriage; he didn't. He said it was a hopeless cause. So I changed my mind and said enough was enough! Then he decided we should try harder; I agreed with him. But then he gave up completely. By now I knew our marriage needed a miracle, and I believed a miracle could still happen if we didn't give up.

"What should I do?" I moaned to my friends. The entire sordid affair was consuming me.

"Joanna," one of them said, "every time we see you, you are more and more dead inside." They prayed with me, and we looked at Scripture verses together. One of the passages I loved speaks of God's protection during severe trials:

> When you pass through the waters, I will be with you; and when you pass through the rivers, they will not sweep over you. When you walk through the fire, you will not be burned; the flames will not set you ablaze. For I am the LORD, your God, the Holy One of Israel, your Savior.... You are precious and honored in my sight.
>
> —ISAIAH 43:2–4

I clung to God and earnestly prayed for a solution. Above everything else, I wanted His will for my life. Eventually I went to see my pastor and his wife. "What do you think I should do?" I asked after pouring out my problems.

I expected them to chastise me for having made such a mess of things. Instead, they showed compassion and concern, prayed for me, and gave me wise counsel. "Joanna, God loves you with an everlasting love. Trust in Him to lead you as you take whatever steps are necessary."

Ted finally filed for divorce. As part of the divorce settlement, we split our accumulated debt, which seemed huge to me. "How will I ever pay this off?" I wondered. When my friend Ann offered to let me live with her, I moved out of the apartment and stayed there a few months until the divorce became final.

Working part-time was no longer an option, and the Lord gave me a full-time job as assistant to a financial consultant. Unfortunately, I also got a shiny new credit card, and I used it to alleviate stress. It may have helped me feel better at the time, but within months I was in more debt than ever. Including a car loan, I now owed seventeen thousand dollars. My salary was barely enough to cover the minimum monthly payments, and at that rate, I would never pay it off. It made me physically ill every time I thought about it.

Yet, Jesus was closer than ever. His daily presence was very real. I was only twenty-three years old and going through the devastation of divorce, but I knew God was personalizing the words of Scripture for me: "The LORD will call you back as if you were a wife deserted and distressed in spirit—a wife who married young, only to be rejected" (Isa. 54:6).

When my church decided to sponsor a two-week missions trip to Scotland, eight of us (all in our twenties) signed up to go. We went to Glasgow to walk the streets and pray. A start-up church needed a permanent location to hold worship services and house their leadership school. I had heard how experiences like that changed people's lives, but in my case, being used of God in that way brought profound inner healing as well. I felt like a new person.

On the return trip home, I dedicated my life completely to Jesus—my husband. I sensed God telling me that there was more to do in Scotland, but that I had to get rid of my financial obligations first.

For the next two years, I prayed and cried many tears. I practically begged God to let me go back to Scotland. He had blessed me with new vision and purpose. My friends Scott and Kelly, members of my discipleship small group, offered to let me live with them so I could keep my expenses down. I moved into their house in September, worked my full-time job during the day, and washed their dishes and played with their three kids at night. I sold all my possessions and put every penny I earned toward paying down my debt. By April I was debt free! On June 1, I was Glasgow-bound, and this time I would stay for a year.

Sitting on the plane that day with pillows and blankets snuggled around me, I had a smile on my face and tears in my eyes. It had been four years since my divorce, and looking back, I could see how Jesus had rescued me, provided for me, and healed my broken heart. He had worked many miracles in my life, and now He was making it possible to serve Him in a beautiful and faraway land.

I reached into my carry-on bag and took out my well-worn Bible. With heartfelt love and gratitude to Jesus, I wept over these words:

> My lover spoke and said to me, "Arise, my darling, my beautiful one, and come with me. See! The winter is past; the rains are over and gone. Flowers appear on the earth; the season of singing has come, the cooing of doves is heard in our land.... Arise, come, my darling; my beautiful one, come with me."
>
> —Song of Solomon 2:10–13

Scotland was wonderful, and I even attended their leadership college—something I never thought I would have the courage to do. I could sense Jesus's presence in and around me, loving me, building my confidence, and maturing my faith in Him.

Back home again, I got a great job working in the office of a burgeoning construction company. Through them I got my Realtor's license, and when I could afford it, I bought a house. I asked my friend Maggie to be my roommate.

Four and a half years later, God gave me a job with a real estate broker. I built a three-bedroom, Craftsman-style house, brick red with khaki-colored trim. I lived alone again for a while and then invited my friend Cordelia to room with me. I rented out my original house.

God continues to manage my life and career, and at age thirty-five I am starting to think of myself as an up-and-coming businesswoman. I have many wonderful friends and a great church, and I own two homes. I can go zip-lining all day and then come home, look across my backyard in search of an occasional duck, bunny, or great blue heron, and whisper thanks to Jesus for the life I have been given. I even have my good friend Molly—my springer spaniel—and she looks at me with her big brown eyes in hopes that I will rub her tummy.

Guiding Principles

A Pinch of Salt

> Do not be in a hurry to get married, especially if you are in your teens or twenties. Wait until more of your values have been solidified and God has had a chance to teach you some important life lessons.

> Let Jesus be the man in your life: your lover, your provider, your friend. Be content in your relationship with Him, and let Him guide your decisions. You do not need a man in your life in order to be whole.

> As good as it feels to wallow and fester in anger, remember that it's better to forgive and pray blessings on the person who wronged you. Anger and unforgiveness not only cause bitterness, but they also hamper your relationship with God. "For if you forgive men when they sin against you, your heavenly Father will also forgive you. But if you do not forgive men their sins, your Father will not forgive your sins" (Matt. 6:14–15).

> Make the necessary sacrifices to get out and stay out of debt. Being in debt is a bondage. It makes you feel miserable and keeps you from living with the freedom and joy God intends for you.

> Know exactly how much money you bring in, and do not let your expenses exceed that amount. Save ahead of time for big expenditures, and don't give in to impulse buying. Avoid the temptation to think, "I want it; I need it; I deserve it...now!"

> Develop a sincere appreciation for good Christian friends. It takes time and effort to maintain relationships, but it adds a dimension to life that cannot be duplicated. Remember too that friendship works both ways. To have a friend, you have to *be* a friend.

> "Take delight in the LORD, and he will give you your heart's desires. Commit everything you do to the LORD. Trust him, and he will help you" (Ps. 37:4–5, NLT). Who knows the desires of your heart better than Jesus does?

Homemade With Heart

One of Joanna's Favorite Recipes

I like to cook, and I have several great recipes. Because I am single, I look for recipes that I can double and then freeze in smaller portions for later use. My sister-in-law taught me how to make burritos, and when I was in Scotland, I made these for the students at the leadership college.

Bravado Burritos

½ rotisserie chicken (or cut up 2 baked chicken breasts)
1 pkg. (8) burrito-sized tortillas
1 can (16 oz.) refried beans
1 pkg. (16 oz.) grated cheese
1 can (15 oz.) black olives, sliced
1 can (4 oz.) diced green chilies
1 can (15 oz.) enchilada sauce

Toppings
Salsa
Sour cream

Avocado chunks or guacamole

Prepare chicken by pulling off and cutting up the meat into bite-sized pieces (or cut up 2 baked chicken breasts).

Make one burrito at a time, making sure to reserve some of the cheese, olives, and green chilies for spreading over the top.

Spread refried beans in a line down the center of the tortilla.

Add a handful of chicken pieces.

Add shredded cheese, sliced olives, and diced green chilies.

Wrap the tortilla like a burrito (fold the two sides inward, then roll up).

Place all burritos in greased baking pans (or freeze some of the burritos for later use). Pour enchilada sauce over the burritos. Top with remaining cheese, olives, and green chilies.

Bake at 400°F for 30–40 minutes until hot throughout (may also be microwaved). Serve hot with toppings.

Now for an Update

With a Cherry on Top

Joanna is a licensed real estate agent and will soon have her broker's license. Not only is she staying out of debt, but she is also building equity and adding to the retirement account she started in her late twenties. As a background vocalist on a worship team at church, she went on a short-term missions trip to Ecuador, and she is learning to play the guitar. Her life is full, never boring—and that's the way she and Jesus like it.

Four

Marinate in Mercy

T O *MARINATE* IS TO SOAK MEAT, FISH, FOWL, OR VEGETABLES IN a liquid that has been enhanced with herbs and spices. In doing so, extra flavor will permeate it before it's cooked or baked. How pleasing it is to God when we saturate—marinate—*ourselves* in His mercy. Over time, we are transformed and become a reflection of His love. Our whole demeanor changes, and then we are able to demonstrate to others the love and mercy God has shown to us.

In "Set the Prisoner Free," Lis Haus had to choose between holding on to the bad memories that resulted from her husband's unfaithfulness and setting aside her forty-year-old hurt. Some would say she had every right to embrace her old grudge, but she decided to ask God what He might have in store.

Hope Rutledge had to show compassion, common sense, and bravery in the decisions she had to make. In "Forging Our Way," she tells how, after a short and fragile marriage, she earned her teaching credentials while raising her small boys. The threesome went on to help pioneer two Christian Farm communities in northern Canada.

When we wander in the desert with little sustenance, we are all the more apt to call out to God. In "God, I Need Help," Linda Heaner was slow to see God's mercy for her family and, like the Israelites, was tempted to complain and reject His not-so-glamorous provision. She asked Him to meet their needs in a more palatable way.

The ability to accept God's grace for ourselves, show love and mercy to others, and heal from a broken past is impossible in human terms. Like a good marinade, there is not a quick fix—time and patience are required. But once we let God's mercy permeate us through and through, it flavors our lives and infiltrates all of our relationships. In the end, it enables us to live much fuller lives than we could have ever imagined.

Set the Prisoner Free

A conversation with Elisabeth Haus

To forgive is to set a prisoner free and discover the prisoner is you.[1]

—LEWIS B. SMEDES

"Lis? It's me, Paul."

Forty-five years had passed since I had heard his voice—forty-five years since he walked out of my life, since he married another woman and started a new family.

"Lis, are you there?"

Why was he calling? Why now? My lips shaped words, and sound followed as if someone else was speaking. "Yes. I'm here."

"I...I know it has been a long time, and...and a lot of water has gone under the bridge, but I was wondering...if maybe we could meet...for dinner?"

Meet for dinner? What did he want? I had made a life for myself, and I didn't want to be hurt again.

Paul had first caught my eye when I was with my family at a lake resort in Michigan. His dark good looks were stunning. He was twenty-two. I was fifteen. It took me five more years to land that handsome fellow, but on a fresh April day we were married.

Within weeks Paul started to hang out at a local bar with his drinking buddies who were still single. Shapely young women swarmed around his bar stool and invited him home with them. I overheard friends say he accepted their invitations, and he didn't deny it when I confronted him.

Our first baby was born, a cherub-cheeked little boy who looked a lot like his daddy. I yearned for Paul to spend time with our son and me, but he continued to spend his evenings at the bar, drinking and slow dancing. When he did come home, it was well past midnight, and the next morning he would sleep in and not get to work on time. His dependence on alcohol had already cost him at least one job. I was afraid he would lose his new job too.

Worry knotted my stomach and sapped me of energy. My fears multiplied when I realized I was pregnant a second time. Even though I was thrilled at the thought of a new little one, I wondered how we would pay our bills. Paul's paychecks met the rent and bought a few groceries, but I couldn't make our money stretch any further.

After our little girl was born, I wondered if having two children would make a difference in Paul's attitude. "Now will my husband settle into family life?" I wondered. I was naïve enough to hope so. But over the next few months, I came to the realization that Paul was not ready to change into *my* image of a faithful family man. I feared if we continued to live together, there would be too many mouths to feed.

One rainy afternoon when the children were napping, I asked him, "What will I do if you lose your job? What will I do if you stop coming home?"

Paul shrugged his shoulders. "Aw, Lis, you know I will always come back eventually."

Even then I could smell the alcohol on his breath. His words, as usual, brought little comfort. In fact, they made me furious, but soon the baby woke up and my mood softened.

I wiped milk from the baby's chin and cuddled her close. I yearned for a marriage that would measure up to the vows we made before God. But I was scared. My mind raced through a litany of doomsday possibilities. I thought, "How will I provide for our family? Will the grocery store extend credit? Can I keep up with the heating bills?" The winter was supposed to be unusually cold. I could almost feel the icy stillness of the house if we ran out of fuel.

For three and a half years I scraped to pay the bills. There was little food in the cupboard but always plenty of beer in the refrigerator. I worried that I might get pregnant again. Finally, I couldn't take the tension any longer. I paced the floor and practiced what I would say when Paul got home. I hoped he would be sober. I wanted him to remember what I was going to tell him.

At last I heard the front door open. He had been drinking, but he wasn't drunk. "Unless you straighten out, I can't take you back anymore," I said. "I'm tired of waiting for you to grow up and settle down."

Paul stared at me for a long time. I didn't know what he was thinking. He stuffed his hands into his pockets and walked back outside.

One day as the kids and I were visiting my parents' house, the papers arrived. Paul had filed for divorce. A relentless rainstorm pounded down on everything that afternoon, and I looked to the sky. "Where are You?" I asked God. "I need Your strength and solace." I felt only weakness and defeat as I shared the news with my parents.

"What am I going to do?" I asked my mother as she finished a game of patty-cake with my little one. She handed the baby to my father. The brightness of our visit had suddenly diminished, and Mom gave me a long, hard hug. Even though I had issued my husband an ultimatum, that did not mean I wanted to lose him. It was the worst day of my life.

With the divorce papers in hand, I was forced to face reality. I looked for a small apartment, but in the early '50s, landlords refused to rent to single women with children. I checked all over town, but the answer was always the same. "I'm sorry, there isn't anything available for you."

My effort at independence had failed. I faced the fact that I needed to accept help, and I went back to my parents. They welcomed the children and me into their house. My kids' earthly father may have abandoned them, but in my parents' home they grew to know God as a Father who would never leave them. In John 14:18, Jesus promises, "I will not leave you as orphans; I will come to you." And in many ways, He did.

I found an assembly job at a nearby factory to support the children and myself. Every morning I left my children in the care of an aunt, who also lived with my parents. I boarded a bus and then walked the remaining three blocks to work. Even though circumstances forced me to accept help from my family, that job gave me a sense of pride and satisfaction. I settled into work and enjoyed the kids as they grew.

After a few years, a terrible loneliness set in, and I longed for male companionship. But I could not shake off the sanctity of my marriage vows, so I refused to bring other men into my life or the lives of my children while they were growing up. I resolutely accepted those years of emptiness—until after the kids were grown. "Now it's time for me," I decided. "It's time to start again."

I developed a friendship with a man who lived nearby and attended my church. Walter often picked me up for Sunday Mass or stopped by just to talk. For eighteen years he was a welcome companion in my life. I was heartbroken when he suffered a stroke and died.

Every once in a while, I would hear some information about Paul. According to friends, he had moved to a distant town, remarried, and raised a new family. I heard that his drinking continued until his wife and children said he had to quit or they would leave. Then he overcame his addiction to alcohol and raised his children.

Paul and his wife had just entered their golden years when she became ill and died. He was alone and spent years in an empty house. His only comfort was the visits from his children.

Then one day I got a phone call from my sister. "You'll never guess who called me just now," she said.

"I can't imagine. Who?"

"It was Paul! He said he noticed our brother's obituary in the paper last week. He offered his condolences, and then he asked, 'How is Lis doing? Do you think she would talk to me if I called her?' So what do you think, sis?" my sister asked. "Do you want to talk to him?"

Decades of my life—a life without Paul—flashed through my mind. "What does he want?" I wondered. "Why is he calling?" My heart and my head were in rebellion. I struggled for a clear thought.

Before I realized what I was saying, words blurted out of my mouth: "Give him my phone number." Then I wasn't sure of the next step, but I was curious to find out the thoughts on his mind after so much time.

In less than an hour Paul called and asked me out to dinner. A lot of time had passed. Did he want us to pick up where we had left off? Just what were his expectations? I needed to find out.

So I accepted the invitation, and a few nights later we faced each other across a small table at a little restaurant near my house. The candle on the table offered a conciliatory glow. We talked into the night. The years had mended many of my hurts, but some of the old wounds opened and bled. Surprisingly, the old attraction we felt when we were young was still there, and we decided to keep on seeing each other.

We frequently argued when one of us tried to make the other understand a point of view. After a while, we realized that neither of us could win the old battles. Forgiveness and understanding needed a place in our lives if there was to be any chance for reconciliation.

My trust in Paul had shattered years ago, and I needed time to reacquaint myself with an alcohol-free, trustworthy companion. When he honored his word and returned to my door consistently, I found that the new Paul was the man I had fallen in love with at that lake resort so many years ago. I was ready to start again.

We spent carefree days at my house in the city and at Paul's home in a small town sixty miles away. We passed summer afternoons side by side in his garden; and when the sun sank low after supper, we strolled the sidewalks together. Small talk and laughter felt so good.

One night Paul squeezed my hand and said, "Let's go to the jewelry store so I can buy you a wedding ring."

I sucked in my breath, barely able to grasp his words. God had answered a prayer I had relinquished many years ago. Now with time and forgiveness on our side, He was restoring our marriage.

Paul and I spent four wonderful years together before he opted for surgery to correct an aortic aneurysm. The operation was successful, but the side effects of anesthesia never permitted him to communicate with anyone again. After the hospital stay, he was discharged to a nursing home where he fell, broke his hip, and died soon afterward. I was heartbroken again, but God offered comfort through the presence of all our children who gathered for final good-byes.

As I look back on my life, I am grateful Paul and I worked together to let go of old grudges so we could forgive and begin anew. I have been truly blessed.

Guiding Principles

A Pinch of Salt

> ➤ When disaster strikes, tackle the practical issues in your life, such as shelter and employment, one step at a time. Trying to solve all your problems at once is a heavy burden.

> Talk to God every day. That's what He is there for. "Praise the LORD, O my soul; all my inmost being, praise his holy name" (Ps. 103:1). "Give thanks to the LORD, for he is good; his love endures forever" (Ps. 118:1).

> If your family and friends offer help, put your pride behind you and accept it. Someday you will regain your independence.

> Ask God to help you to forgive and to set your spirit free.

Homemade With Heart

One of Lis's Favorite Recipes

I have grandchildren who live all across the country, so when everyone comes home, there is good reason to celebrate. When the Haus family gets together, everyone pitches in, including me. I love to bring a big bowl of Jell-O salad. With just four ingredients to buy, it's quick and easy. Best of all, it is sweet enough to serve as a dessert if one is needed.

Lis's Lime Jell-O Salad

1 pkg. (3 oz.) lime Jell-O
1 cup boiling water
1 can (20 oz.) crushed pineapple (drain juice and set aside)
½ cup cold water
1 pkg. (8 oz.) cream cheese (chilled and chopped into bite-sized pieces)
1 container whipped topping

Shake Jell-O into a large bowl or a 9 x 13 inch pan. Add boiling water and stir until Jell-O dissolves (about 3 minutes).

Add cold water and ½ cup of the drained pineapple juice to the Jell-O. Stir for 2 minutes. Add the pineapple and cream cheese. Stir to combine. Refrigerate for 1 hour.

Fold in whipped topping. Chill for several hours or overnight.

Now for an Update

With a Cherry on Top

Today Lis lives alone. She beams in the sunshine of her children, grandchildren, and her first great-grandchild. She continues to rely on the strength she receives in prayer, and she rejoices in a God who blessed her later years with a fully restored marriage.

Forging Our Way

A conversation with Hope Rutledge

> For I know the thoughts that I think toward you, saith the LORD, thoughts of peace, and not of evil, to give you an expected end.
> —JEREMIAH 29:11, KJV

The Farm community seemed a long way off, but I kept driving in my rental car. I flew from Minneapolis to Edmonton, Alberta, then continued my journey with more than five hundred miles of highway, finishing the last few miles over bumpy dirt roads. Hills dotted with trees hid an abundance of wildlife: lynx, fox, deer, moose, and bear. Now I was getting close!

My foot stepped harder on the accelerator, and catching sight of the red and white barn, I called out, "Hello, *home!*" I had not been here for five years, and the tightness in my throat told me I had missed the place more than I realized.

Pulling the car to the side of the road, I got out for a long look around. The community lay in the valley below, a river curled along the edge of town. Two or three log cabins had been added. Trees and lawns were a lush green, and I focused my gaze on the gardens that were no doubt teeming with giant beets, carrots, potatoes, and cabbages sweeter than anything you could find in a store.

This Farm community, and others like it, had been founded in the early 1970s by Christians homesteading in northern Canada. My little family of three was among them.

Twelve years before, my husband, Bruce, and I had started married life in British Columbia, about two hundred miles north of the Cascade Mountains. Bruce was Canadian and a teacher at the high school. The apartment we lived in was part of a large home that had been converted into six apartments.

After being married for a number of years and having two children, David (age three) and Josh (fourteen months), I was at home one day, packing our winter clothes away for the summer. As I reached down to straighten the quilt at the bottom of a big trunk, my hands felt something square and hard. Turning back the edge of the blanket, I discovered a plaque hidden underneath. It read:

> Thanks for teaching us.
> Good luck in your new ventures.

The plaque obviously belonged to my husband, but what could it mean? Had he quit his job without telling me? That night I asked him to explain.

"Teaching is too much pressure for me," he said. "I'm going to work odd jobs this summer, then maybe by fall I will know what to do."

A feeling of dread came over me, and I began to realize my marriage was not what I had hoped. I watched and prayed that my husband would feel better while I continued to care for the boys. Over the next few weeks, I lost thirty pounds as I watched my marriage fail.

When autumn arrived, the thought of once again taking on the full-time responsibility of a wife and children was still too much pressure for my husband. "I have to go away," he said.

I was stunned.

Now out of money, I prayed long and hard about what to do. I decided to take David and Josh with me and drive down to Washington State to look for work. (Because I was an American citizen, I couldn't work in Canada.) I thought it would be relatively easy to add a teaching certification to my English degree, and then I would be able to support my family.

After pursuing several options, I received a teaching fellowship to work on my master's degree. I rented a cottage on a lake near the college campus and scheduled all my classes for Mondays, Wednesdays, and Fridays so I could be at home with the boys as much as possible.

Before long, Bruce came after us. He moved close by but still on the north side of the Canadian border. Some days he appeared without warning, followed us in his car, or stopped in for a visit. He told me the boys were in danger—he didn't think I could take care of them—and he thought they might die. He threatened to take them faraway where he would find a cave for them to live in and be safe from the world.

One afternoon I came home to find the house eerily quiet. I noticed a handwritten note on the kitchen table, grabbed it, and read the babysitter's scrawl: "The boys' dad came and took them for a drive."

I drew in my breath with a gasp. "Lord, protect my boys," I said aloud. Immediately I went into prayer, continually pacing the floor back and forth. I clenched my fists, half shouting, half pleading, all the while still praying, "Bring them home, Lord. Bring my boys home."

Some of my favorite Bible verses strengthened me too. "When I am afraid, I will trust in you. In God, whose word I praise, in God I trust; I will not be afraid. What can mortal man do to me?" (Ps. 56:3–4).

An hour later, Bruce's car pulled into the driveway. "Calm down," he told me. "I just took them to buy you a Mother's Day gift." I looked down and saw David holding a brown paper sack in his little hands.

My friends at the college insisted that I see a lawyer to make sure Bruce couldn't take the boys out of the United States. Since Canadian law favored the rights of fathers at that time, I felt I had no other choice than to file for divorce and ask for full custody of the children. Even though it was my right to do so, I did not ask that the boys' dad be required to pay child support; he was not capable of it at the time, and I didn't want to be the cause of him going to jail.

He left us alone after that. A few months later, I got my master's degree, and by then, I knew teaching at the college level was for me. More education was needed in order to do that, so I applied for and received a doctoral fellowship from a university in Tennessee.

I packed our meager belongings into the old station wagon, and the kids and I drove for four days from Washington to Tennessee. I promised the boys a milk shake and a swim every evening if they were good during that day's drive. Once there, I wasted no time in looking for an inexpensive house. Someone had given me a thousand dollars, and I was planning to use the money for a down payment. I had arranged in advance for a Realtor to take us around on our first day there. She bought us lunch (thank goodness), and by nightfall, the boys and I were sleeping on the floor of our very own place.

Three years later, God provided several possible teaching positions to choose from. In northern Canada, a group of Christian friends was planning to establish a small Farm community with their own private school on sixteen hundred acres, and I liked that option the best. It would be a great place for the boys to grow up; they would have men to model their lives after and plenty of kids to share outdoor fun. Best of all, we would be part of a close-knit community engaged in an extraordinary work for the kingdom of God.

It didn't take much to sell my now eleven- and nine-year-old sons on the idea of adventure. They practiced shooting imaginary moose, stalking grizzly bears from behind the furniture, and hooting like owls from their beds at night. We packed up again, this time caravanning with two other families from the southern United States to whatever lay ahead in the northern wilderness.

It was September 25 when we arrived, and others who had arrived earlier were already clearing the land. Log cabins were erected one by one until eventually each family had their own. A log barn was constructed for the cattle, chickens, pigs, grains, and hay. Another log building served as a combination dining hall, church, and school. Over the years, I was teacher, and then principal, to many of the students.

Life was hard, and there was not much money, but we didn't care. David and Josh flourished at the Farm in all the ways healthy boys do. We were an integral part of the large Christian group, but we had our private times too. We perfected three-way hugs, made great music on our beat-up guitars, and sang our hearts out on spirited songs like "Will the Circle Be Unbroken" and "Kum Ba Yah."

I tried to establish family traditions for our little threesome, and perhaps one of the most innovative was what I called "Christmas breakfast in a sock." I bought the largest men's work socks I could find, and after the boys were asleep on Christmas Eve, I filled them with foods they liked. I would drape a bulging sock across the foot of each bed, including my own so I could act surprised. Inside the socks were hard-boiled eggs, peeled and sliced in half, dotted with butter, sprinkled with salt and pepper, and covered with plastic wrap. Toothpicks—red and green when we had them—held the two halves together.

We also found mandarin oranges inside our socks, and two or three pieces of homemade baking. Each year I tried a different recipe, and we would talk about whatever country it originated from—German *stollen* or *pfeffernusse*, Norwegian *yulekage*, or braided bread shaped like a wreath from Sweden. Sometimes I put other delicacies in the socks too, but without fail I threw in several handfuls of unshelled mixed nuts. I never told the kids, but I liked watching them struggle to crack those open during the rest of the day.

After living and teaching at the Farm for eight years, I moved southeast to another Farm community where they were expanding their school to include college students. By then David and Josh were ready to be on their own, so I became housemother to students living in a dormitory-style cabin. Many times the Scripture verse came to mind that says, "And all thy children shall be taught of the LORD; and great shall be the peace of thy children" (Isa. 54:13, KJV).

Everyone worked hard at this Farm community, just as they had at the previous one. Here there were twenty-five hundred acres to tend, and since there were twice as many families, there was more of everything to do. Every morning at 7:30, we gathered for devotions. On Wednesdays and Sundays we had rousing worship services filled with praises for what the Lord was doing in our midst. Meals were served family style in the dining hall; when the bell rang, everyone would quit whatever they were doing and go there to eat.

As a single mother and teacher, I learned to depend on God with all my might, just like the Lord told Joshua when he came to the Promised Land: "Do not let this Book of the Law depart from your mouth; meditate on it day and night, so that you may be careful to do everything written in it. Then you will be prosperous and successful. Have I not commanded you? Be strong and courageous. Do not be terrified; do not be discouraged, for the LORD your God will be with you wherever you go" (Josh. 1:8–9).

The dinner bell started ringing and brought an end to my reminiscing at the top of the hill. I glanced at my watch. It was dinnertime, all right. Maybe I would surprise everyone and sneak in on them while they had their eyes closed in prayer. My heart leapt at the idea, and I jumped into my car for the short ride *home.*

Guiding Principles

A Pinch of Salt

> Identify the skills you have already acquired, and seek ways to build on them. When you persevere in your goals, you multiply your options. "The LORD your God is with you, he is mighty to save. He will take great delight in you, he will quiet you with his love, he will rejoice over you with singing" (Zeph. 3:17).

> Appreciate every answer to prayer that you receive— even small steps forward. "If the LORD delights in a man's way, he makes his steps firm; though he stumble, he will not fall, for the LORD upholds him with his hand" (Ps. 37:23–24). Think of your progress as a mile-post pointing you toward a safe, satisfying destination, and make sure your accomplishments glorify God. He loves you and grants you the privilege of serving Him.

> Do not make decisions quickly or totally on your own. Get valuable input from family and friends to check and confirm your own inclinations. Also confer with others about your family's health and progress from time to time. Make sure you are heading in the right direction and are staying on course.

Homemade With Heart

One of Hope's Favorite Recipes

I used to make *yulekage* (a Norwegian Christmas bread pronounced *YOOL kah gah*) from a yeast dough, but as delicious as that is, it takes a lot of time and energy. Now I buy the frozen bread dough and add my fruits and nuts to that. Scented with cardamom, threaded with candied fruit, and topped with a vanilla frosting, you can serve *yulekage* for any occasion, not just at Christmas, and certainly not just in a sock.

Easy Yulekage (Christmas Bread)

2 loaves frozen white bread dough
   (or make dough using your favorite yeast sweet roll recipe)
½ tsp. ground cardamom (or more to taste)
1 tsp. grated lemon zest
½ cup mixed candied fruit, diced
½ cup golden raisins and/or craisins (optional)
½ cup walnut pieces

Frosting
¾ cup powdered sugar
1 Tbsp. water
1 tsp. vegetable oil
½ tsp. almond extract

Thaw frozen bread dough according to package directions. To speed the process, heat the oven to 200°F, turn oven off, and place the dough inside to keep warm.

Knead the loaves together on a lightly floured work surface until soft. Flatten the dough with your hands, distribute the cardamom, lemon zest, candied fruit, raisins, craisins, and walnut pieces on top, and thoroughly work them in.

Transfer to a large greased bowl and set aside to rise until doubled in size (one or two hours).

Punch down and knead dough, ending with a circle shape. Place in a 9-inch round cake pan, lightly greased. Press firmly so the dough fills the pan evenly. Cover with a towel and set aside to rise until the dough again doubles in size (about 45 minutes).

Preheat the oven to 350°F. Bake for about 45 minutes or until golden brown.

Mix together all frosting ingredients and frost when the round loaf is cooled. Decorate with maraschino cherries and walnuts or pecans if desired. Best served warm or toasted, with butter.

Now for an Update

With a Cherry on Top

Hope taught at the Farm communities for twenty-three years, even after her boys grew to be young men and moved to the United States to pursue their education and careers. She eventually left Canada to be closer to her sons and grandchildren, but she continues to teach part-time at several nearby Bible schools and colleges.

God, I Need Help

A conversation with Linda Joyce Heaner

I will strengthen you and help you; I will uphold you with
my righteous right hand.
—ISAIAH 41:10

"Why aren't You helping me?" I asked the Lord. "Christians aren't
supposed to get divorced!"

I paced my living room and prayed. I had hoped a six-month separation would restore our faltering marriage. I stayed in the apartment
with our children—Timothy, six; Rachel, three; and Jonathan, one—
and trusted God to work a miracle. I fully expected a reconciliation
of our relationship.

Money had been scarce in our household for years. When my
husband moved out, I needed immediate help because I had no job
and no savings. I *had* to find a way to care for my three children.
With deep reservations, I applied for government assistance through a
program called Aid to Families with Dependent Children (AFDC).

Immediately I felt tremendous guilt. "What's wrong with me, Lord?"
I asked Him over and over. "Why can't I provide for my children some
other way?" I hated a program that made me feel as if I was a number
instead of a person. It was a sterile system, sorely lacking in compassion. In deep, agonizing prayer I asked God for a better solution.

"This is part of My provision for you *at this time*," God seemed to
say. This was a totally new way of looking at it. Now I could accept
this financial help as coming from God, and I could thank Him for it,
even if others might look down on me for receiving it.

Accepting help allowed me to be home with my three young children. I wanted to raise them to love and serve the Lord, so I did my

best to trust Him and accept the drastic changes in my life. I worked as a freelance writer and provided in-home children's day care to earn as much as possible without losing benefits provided by the government. Soon I was amazed at other forms of assistance God offered me. He brought additional resources through personal friends, social organizations, local churches, and scholarships. Other help came in the way of food stamps, food shelves, and rent assistance.

A few months after my husband moved out, I was served with divorce papers that stated we had *irreconcilable differences*. Those two words did not make sense to me.

By now we had been separated for seventeen months. With our court date in three weeks, I still thought we could work things out, but I was powerless to fight the no-fault divorce laws of the state we lived in.

"God, how can this be happening? Help me!" I cried out.

Inside my head, I heard God say, "Don't look around at your circumstances. Look at Me! I am your abiding hope."

"Abiding hope? What does that mean?" I wondered. "I don't understand, Lord, but I'll hang on to Your words." Sadly, my eleven-year marriage ended.

Though I was grateful for God's ongoing provision for my children and me, I still looked forward to the day when I would no longer be on assistance and could pay my own way. I was so focused on the practical issues of day-to-day survival that I had not noticed how fragile my emotional health was.

Two years following the divorce, my pastor's wife died after a long illness. The church was filled to capacity with friends and acquaintances mourning the loss of a beautiful woman. I sat alone in the pew, noticing how supportive everyone was to our pastor.

It made me think of the similarities between death and divorce. The loss can be every bit as permanent and devastating either way—even though society barely notices when a divorce occurs.

When the service was over for the pastor's wife, everyone headed for the graveside service at the cemetery. Unable to find someone to ride with, I drove alone. On the way, I burst into tears, and before I knew what was happening, my whole body was wracked with giant sobs that turned into wailing that would not stop.

"What is going on here?" I wondered as I continued to weep. "This is about more than my friend's death!" I could not stop comparing her funeral to my divorce.

Days later, a deep sadness still hung over me—so much so that I confided in a close friend. "I know this sounds trite, Linda," my friend Gretchen told me, "but Jesus was there with you *during* your divorce." Her words made me cry again.

The next day I spent extended time alone with God and brought Him my aching heart. "Father, please help me face these feelings," I prayed. "Show me the truth." Immediately a scene flashed through my mind:

> *I am driving to the cemetery for the burial of my marriage. I am totally alone; no one else has come with me to witness the interment, to comfort or support me. No one is here to encourage me or reassure me of God's love. I arrive alone, pay my respects alone, leave alone, drive home alone, and cry alone. Oh, Lord, how I hurt inside!*

Then I saw the same scene again, but it was different this time:

> *I am driving to the cemetery for the burial of my marriage. Jesus is sitting in the front seat beside me. He doesn't say a word, but His eyes tell me that He feels my pain. When we arrive, Jesus takes my hand and walks with me to the grave site.*

My pain is so deep. I feel like I'm being ripped to pieces and that part of me is dying and being buried. I begin to sob uncontrollably. Jesus turns to me, and I bury my head in His shoulder. He gently and compassionately holds me close. I cry about my broken hopes and dreams, I cry in anger that I could not stop the divorce from happening, and I cry over the responsibility of caring for my three small children. Then I cry about my fears of the future, I cry over the searing pain of rejection, and I cry because my life is in shambles. I cry until I am completely exhausted.

Slowly I begin to calm down. Then I realize that Jesus has been crying right along with me. He feels my anguish, my despair, and my loss. Gently He cups my face in His hands, then His deep, loving eyes look right into mine. "Linda," He says, "I will never leave you or forsake you."

Tenderly Jesus picks me up and carries my limp body to the car. He drives me home, carries me into the house, and helps me get comfortable so I can rest. Time goes on, but Jesus stays.

Day after day, Jesus makes Himself available. Slowly, very slowly, I begin to regain my strength. Yet I am finding that in no way am I outgrowing my constant need for Jesus.[2]

My relationship with God had been strong in my life before my divorce, but I did not realize until afterward how necessary it was to trust in Him completely. I learned that He was eager to provide for my every practical, emotional, and spiritual need.

To this day, if I falter in my faith, He abides: "If we are faithless, he will remain faithful" (2 Tim. 2:13). When I cry out for help, He is there: "I will ask the Father, and He will give you another Helper, that He may be with you forever" (John 14:16, NASU). Best of all, whenever

I begin to pace my living room in despair, I soon remember that He is still my abiding hope: "Let him have all your worries and cares, for he is always thinking about you and watching everything that concerns you" (1 Pet. 5:7, TLB).

Guiding Principles

A Pinch of Salt

> Run to God first. Live in His presence, know His promises, and trust Him no matter what. Be assured that God will be there to guide you, to console you, and to encourage you. "...Because God has said, 'Never will I leave you; never will I forsake you'" (Heb. 13:5).

> Thank God in advance for how He will meet your need. Keep your eyes on Him, not on your situation. Then lean on Him for strength. "So do not fear, for I am with you; do not be dismayed, for I am your God. I will strengthen you and help you; I will uphold you with my righteous right hand" (Isa. 41:10).

> Receive help from other people, organizations, churches, government programs, and scholarships as part of God's provision for you *at this time*. This cultivates gratefulness, not a sense of inadequacy or entitlement. God provides these helps while telling you not to worry. "Do not be anxious about anything, but in everything, by prayer and petition, with thanksgiving, present your requests to God. And the peace of God, which transcends all understanding, will guard your hearts and your minds in Christ Jesus" (Phil. 4:6–7).

> Ask if community programs such as swimming lessons, sporting leagues, and park events offer financial help. Many do, but they do not advertise it.

> Celebrate God's faithfulness to your family with your children and others. "Because of the LORD's great love we are not consumed, for his compassions never fail. They are new every morning; great is your faithfulness" (Lam. 3:22–23).

Homemade With Heart

One of Linda's Favorite Recipes

When my children were little, I made family time a priority, especially during lunch and dinner. A meal is much more than eating; it's about conversation, about sharing the events of the day, and about relationship. A favorite at our house, this recipe—named by the kids—was inexpensive and quick to prepare, but more importantly, it was fun!

Tuna, Noodle, and Grape

1 box (8 oz.) macaroni
1 can tuna, drained
Grapes, sliced in half (amounts can vary)
Mayonnaise (or Miracle Whip) to taste

Cook your favorite macaroni according to package directions. Strain macaroni and combine with one can tuna. Add grapes that have been sliced in half and one grape that has been left whole. Add mayonnaise (or Miracle Whip) to taste.

Let the kids discover who got the one whole grape!

Now for an Update

With a Cherry on Top

One of Linda's greatest joys is that all three of her children (now in their twenties) wholeheartedly love Jesus. All have served as missionaries in various regions of the world through Youth With A Mission (YWAM).

Linda is passionate about restoring hope to single mothers. In 1989 she launched Abiding Hope Ministries, which enables her to offer encouragement, spiritual support, and practical help. The ministry provides a variety of resources and trains others who want to help single moms. Linda speaks at retreats, churches, and conferences and has led support groups for single mothers, homeschooling moms, and women recovering from divorce. Her book, *God, I Need Help*, was published in 2005. For more information about Linda and Abiding Hope Ministries, visit www.abidinghope.com.

Five

Purée Until Peaceful

THE THOUGHT OF BEING PURÉED IS NOT PRETTY, EVEN THOUGH it seems life does that to us sometimes. When tragedy strikes, we feel chopped, mashed, processed, and strained until all that is left of us is a fine pulp. It's OK to purée creamy soups, and it's fun to purée a smoothie, but what about when life's circumstances decide to purée us?

Nancy Brown felt that way when she lost two husbands—both unexpectedly. Although it was not part of her plan, she made the decision to learn "the art of grieving well." Initially angry with God and wanting some answers, she got more than she bargained for.

Great faith is not developed by the faint of heart. When tumult invaded the life of Esther Grafs, she could have either turned her face to the wall or cried out to God for restoration. In Esther we find an inspiring and unforgettable example of a woman who knows that "God is good—all the time."

"He Gives and Takes Away" is Janis Hackman's account of her late-in-life marriage to a widower who was convinced (as was Janis) that God brought them together. When terminal illness struck, they both felt overwhelmed, but Janis tells how the Lord was faithful and brought them to peace in the end.

When life puts us through the blender and then through a sieve, we would do well to remember the age-old definition of *peace*. It is not the absence of suffering, but it's the presence of God. One day when we are in heaven, we will experience that ultimate peace. "Never again will they hunger; never again will they thirst. The sun will not beat upon them, nor any scorching heat. For the Lamb at the center of the throne will be their shepherd; he will lead them to springs of living water. And God will wipe away every tear from their eyes" (Rev. 7:16–17).

The Art of Grieving Well

A conversation with Nancy Brown

I was angry with God and couldn't feel His presence, but I decided to talk to Him anyway and tell Him how I felt.

—NANCY BROWN

The smell of pot roast, potatoes, and carrots coming from the Crock-Pot was making me hungry. By the time I arrived home from my job, Milt had already been there and left. The first thing he liked to do after work was to take a short ride on his bike. It helped relieve the daily stress of serving as pastor in a large metropolitan church. He would be home any minute.

I was setting the table when I heard a racket on the front porch. That couldn't be Milt, could it? I rushed to the door and saw him sprawled next to the steps with his bicycle askew alongside him. He was ghostly pale, his eyes were closed, and his body was trembling.

I didn't know what to do first—go to him or call 9-1-1. In my confusion, I eventually managed to do both. What I remember most about the next horrifying minutes is how I prayed and prayed for Milt to be all right.

The paramedics arrived within minutes with sirens wailing and lights flashing. Everything happened so fast. "Milt is only fifty-seven," I reminded myself. "He is in excellent health, so he can't possibly die."

But he did. Milt never regained consciousness, and I never told him good-bye. Later we discovered that Milt had a heart defect he never knew about.

Shock immediately took over. My brain felt as if it was stuffed with cotton, and I moved like a zombie. For days my four grown children and close friends had to tell me what to do. I was in physical pain. It felt as if broken glass stabbed my skin and huge rubber bands compressed my head and neck. I could not eat or sleep.

When we made the funeral arrangements, we could not decide on which scriptures to use. There were so many that he loved. "Let's look in Dad's journal," my daughter Chrissie suggested. "Maybe we can find a favorite verse there."

Milt's notebook lay on the small table beside his easy chair. His Bible and devotional booklets were stacked there too. Gently, Chrissie lifted Milt's journal from the pile, and, holding it like a sacred relic, she gingerly turned the pages.

"Oh, Mother," she said, hardly able to talk. "Look what Dad wrote that morning before he left for work." He had copied two verses out of the Bible and then wrote comments about them. This is what he wrote:

"So we fix our eyes not on what is seen, but on what is unseen. For what is seen is temporary, but what is unseen is eternal" (2 Cor. 4:18).

Good news! Our troubles will soon be over, but the joys to come will last forever.

"Therefore we are always confident and know that as long as we are at home in the body we are away from the Lord" (2 Cor. 5:6).

What a super attitude. We look forward to our heavenly bodies, realizing every moment we spend in our

 *earthly bodies is time spent away from our eternal home in heaven with Jesus.*

My knees went weak, and I lowered myself into the chair next to his. I covered my face with my hands and sobbed. Had Milt sensed he was about to die? Did God whisper in his ear that He would see him soon?

At the funeral, one of the pastors read Milt's journal entry. It was meant to encourage the congregants in their faith, but I sat in a daze. "How could this happen?" I asked the Lord. "We were married for thirty-four years. He was the love of my life, and I have loved You too. How can You treat me this way?"

My emotions crowded out most of what was said that day. Over the next few days, I constantly remembered how Milt and I enjoyed each other's company, how we prayed together and nurtured one another. We directed Marriage Encounter Weekends together in hopes that other married couples could cultivate the same kind of intimacy we shared.

As more time passed, everyone who knew and loved Milt went back to their normal routines except me. My life would never be normal again. Depression took hold and deepened. Milt's paychecks stopped coming, and I started to worry about finances.

It wasn't long before I had to apply for Social Security death benefits. A friend went with me, and we made our way through downtown traffic to the massive government building. The marble hallways echoed our footsteps, and after a lengthy wait in the appropriate lobby, a clerk called my number and directed us to a cubicle where a man with a bored expression shuffled through a pile of paper.

"When did the marriage end?" he asked after taking down my contact information.

"It didn't end!" I wanted to scream. "See my wedding ring?"

But I restrained myself, and in a raspy monotone barely recognizable to myself, I plodded through the questions on his list. Once that ordeal was over, I had to contend with other financial matters as well. Milt was the one who handled our affairs, but now I had to make myself accountable.

Anger was the primary emotion that took up residence in my heart. Milt's death seemed so unfair. He had been such a loving person—great husband, attentive father, and an excellent pastor. I had loved God from my youth, but now my anger drove me in the opposite direction. I have heard that some people feel very close to God after the death of a loved one, but I did not.

A friend advised me to keep on talking to God despite my feelings, and it turned out to be good advice. A person needs to get their anger out! I made the decision to change churches so I would not have to be reminded of Milt leading the worship services. After a while I started reading the psalms. Many of my emotions were represented there, and that was a comfort. One of the verses that particularly helped me was Psalm 69:3: "I am worn out calling for help; my throat is parched. My eyes fail, looking for my God."

Soon I was reading other Bible passages, and my heart gradually softened. The day finally came when I humbled myself before God and cried, "Lord, forgive me for being so angry with You when all You have shown me is mercy and love."

A year and a half after Milt's death, a friend at my new church asked me to speak at a retreat. What could I possibly have to say with a broken heart still not fully mended? Yet I let myself be persuaded. "You have so much to teach us," she urged, "and it will be good for you."

As I prepared my message for the retreat, words gushed onto the paper. It was as if I were writing a love letter to God. More than once I had the sensation of a warm, soothing ointment healing my aching heart. That emotional breakthrough allowed me to sense God's loving presence once again. I smiled; I sang; it had been months since I showed that kind of enthusiasm and joy. To my amazement, I started entertaining thoughts about a happy future.

Some time after that, I attended a Beginning Experience weekend for Christians. Everyone there was divorced except a widower named Bob and me. Only the two of us had experienced the ravages of death, so I engaged him in conversation to put him at ease. "I lost my wife of thirty-four years to cancer," he told me. "That was a year ago, and the year before, my thirty-year-old daughter also died of cancer."

I expressed my sympathies and asked him about how he had adjusted to such terrible loss. "Not so well," Bob shared as he lowered his eyes and hugged his arms to his chest. "I have been working twelve- to fourteen-hour days on the job, and I bring more work home. If I need to rest or get some sleep, I turn on the television."

We chatted easily, and all the while I was making mental notes about how men process grief differently than women.

"My wife's clothes are still in the closet," he confessed near the end of our conversation. "Most of her things are just like she left them, and I can't bear to take them away."

My heart went out to that big, friendly guy. He seemed so lost, and I wondered how many other men felt the same way.

The next week Bob surprised me with a telephone call. "Can I take you out for dinner?" he asked.

"Oh, I'm not ready to date," I replied. "Thanks anyway, but it's too soon."

He persisted, and I didn't have the heart to turn him down. So finally I agreed, saying, "OK, but just this once."

As soon as we relaxed, we conversed easily, just as we had at the weekend retreat. This time, though, we talked about our personal histories and discovered many things we held in common—teaching, writing, small group leadership, and our values. Bob had a warm personality with a big laugh. When I agreed to "one more dinner date" with Bob, I got a warm, spontaneous hug in return.

It didn't take too many dinners to realize we were falling in love. We felt like teenagers again. My stomach did flip-flops, and there was a permanent smile on my face.

At the same time, I felt a little guilty. What would Milt think? Would he consider my love for Bob a betrayal? What would he say if he knew Bob wanted to marry me?

After days of agony, I took out a piece of stationery and wrote a love letter to Milt. It began: "My dearest, I still love you with all my heart…" Then I told him how I missed him and how grieving his loss was by far the hardest thing I had ever done. I wrote about my adjustment to a new life and that I felt God had given me a new man to love.

I concluded the letter with: "I will always love you, Milt, and I know you would consider my marriage to Bob a blessing."

Only two years after Milt's death, I walked down the aisle with Bob. I had my family's blessing, and they welcomed him into our midst. Bob's children helped him clean, redecorate, and sell his house so he could move into mine.

After we were settled, Bob and I started a grief support ministry we called New Morning Ministries. We wanted to help people recover from loss and start their lives again. People need to talk about their losses. We learned that by focusing on others, we ourselves received healing. We rejoiced in God's plan to put us together.

One morning in April, we sat on the couch making plans for our day. Suddenly a strange look came over Bob's face. He gasped, and his head dropped back. I rushed to his side, calling his name several times. I tried to do CPR, but he was gone.

I grabbed the phone and forced my trembling fingers to punch 9-1-1. Suddenly I was reenacting the night of Milt's death. In my state of confusion, the past intruded on the present, and it was difficult to keep them separated in my mind.

Within minutes the ambulance came for Bob, just as it had for Milt. Sirens wailed; lights flashed. The same paramedics team came. They recognized me from when they tried to save Milt six years before. Despite their efforts, Bob could not be revived. Death had struck again.

I knew Bob had a heart condition when we married four years earlier, but when he went for his regular checkups, the doctor said he was fine. He was overweight, but we were working on that. Maybe I should have insisted he stay on a strict diet.

After Bob's death, I didn't feel the same anger toward God that I carried after Milt's, but my depression was deeper and lasted longer. Many times I asked God, "Why did I have to lose two husbands?" Many prayers later, I seemed to hear God say, "Can you trust Me even if I never tell you why?"

I stopped whining. He didn't have to tell me anything. When Job questioned God's motives, the Lord didn't give him a direct answer (Job 38–40). I humbled myself and asked God to forgive my impertinence.

A few days later, these words came clearly to my mind: "I allowed this because I trust you." I knew God had spoken to my spirit, and a peaceful assurance settled over me.

As soon as I could, I went back to leading the grief support group that Bob and I had started. Much of my healing came from that atmosphere of understanding and love. Twice I was an unwilling inductee into the widow's club. For months I felt as if I had a big, black *W* on my chest. But I have learned from my experiences, and I am determined to help others.

Grief is not supposed to last forever.

Once in a while, I wonder how the Lord might be trusting me. Was it with Bob's healing from the double loss he suffered before we met? Am I to help dozens, maybe even hundreds, of people through their grieving processes? I am beginning to see this happen already.

Whatever God has in mind for me, I don't think He wants me to slack off during my retirement years. I know He is trusting me for things, and I choose to trust Him too.

Guiding Principles

A Pinch of Salt

> Decide to walk through grief with grace. Embrace your pain and look to God for comfort and help.

> Expect grief to take you on a journey through denial, isolation, anger, bargaining, and depression (not necessarily in that order). Do not be discouraged when you think you have finished with one of the stages and it comes around again. After grief has run its course, you will come to the place of acceptance.

> Get adequate rest. Grief takes a tremendous amount of energy. Treat yourself like an injured patient who needs good care, good nutrition, fresh air, and friends.

> Look for a surprise in each day, and try to see the love of God in it: a phone call from a friend, a special memory that comes to mind, or colorful clouds in the sky.

> Journal about your feelings instead of stuffing them. Spill your emotions onto the page. If you are afraid someone might see what you wrote, ask a trusted friend to discard your journal at the appropriate time. (If I die before I wake, throw my journal in the lake.)

> Look for a grief support group, and use the following criteria as a checklist:

- [ ] There is an atmosphere of trust and confidentiality.
- [ ] The facilitator keeps the discussion moving and does not let one person dominate.
- [ ] Everyone is given a chance to talk.
- [ ] Group members are encouraged to be good listeners and refrain from giving advice.
- [ ] Problems that have been solved are shared as "one possible way" to do it.
- [ ] People with serious problems are referred to a trained counselor.
- [ ] Membership for the sole purpose of finding a new mate is discouraged.
- [ ] Members sign an agreement promising confidentiality.

Homemade With Heart

One of Nancy's Favorite Recipes

Milt loved to take me to the Pannekoeken Restaurant, where the waitresses literally *ran* from the kitchen to your table shouting, "Pannekoeken!" (*PAN-ah-koo-kin*). When I found the recipe and started making it at home, I tried to replicate the running and shouting but had limited success. It gave us a good laugh, though, and became a family favorite.

Pannekoeken (Dutch Pancakes) for Two

Powdered sugar
½ cup blueberries (or a similar fruit)
½ cup milk
½ cup flour

4 eggs
3 Tbsp. butter

Preheat oven to 400°F. Dust blueberries with powdered sugar and set aside.

Mix milk, flour, and eggs in a blender.

Melt butter in a deep 10-inch, cast-iron skillet by placing it in the oven (make sure the handle is ovenproof). Remove the skillet briefly and swirl the melted butter until it covers the pan's surface. Add the egg mixture to the hot skillet. Drop in the berries or other fruit. Bake for 20 minutes.

When the pancake is puffy and brown, remove it from the oven and call out, "Pannekoeken!" Serve it quickly while hot with Cool Whip, pancake syrup, or vanilla yogurt.

Now for an Update

With a Cherry on Top

Nancy has written and published a book called *Suddenly Your World Falls Apart: A Guide to Grieving Well*.[1] "I have been given a brand-new career through this book," Nancy says. "And ministering the grace of God has become my passionate plan for life." Nancy continues to lead the grief support group at her church and has been invited to do radio and television interviews. She has also taken seminary courses and earned a pastoral degree in counseling and spiritual direction.

When Dennis Brown, one of Bob's best friends, joined her grief group a few years ago, Nancy found another loving partner, and they were married in 2003. "He is a very brave man," she says with humor.

God Is Good—All the Time

A conversation with Esther Grafs

Give thanks to the LORD, for he is good; his love endures forever.

—PSALM 118:1

Henry and I were married for fifty-three years. It was not easy, but it's not the easy things that keep us dependent on God.

We didn't plan to raise seventeen children—four biological and thirteen adopted. The Lord just sent them to us. At first we tried foster care, but parting with the kids was too heart wrenching. I cried myself to sleep after each child left.

Finally one night, I rolled over in bed and grabbed a tissue from the nightstand. I said to my husband, "I can't do this anymore. I can't love them and hug them, wipe their chins and bottoms, and then let them go." With that, I made the decision to quit taking in children no matter how desperately they needed time away from their troubled families.

But it didn't take long before I missed the little ones. I even longed for the sullen teenagers who yearned for their own kind of acceptance. "Can't we just adopt some of these kids?" I asked Henry.

"I've been thinking the same thing," he said. "We have the room, and they sure need a family." We called our contact at the social services agency and told her that instead of providing foster care for children, we wanted to adopt them. When I hung up the phone, I felt as if I had plugged a leak in my heart. Now when the kids came, there would not be the nagging dread of having to eventually let them go.

We already had five kids in the house—our four and a nephew whose parents could no longer care for him. Within weeks of declaring our new status with the agency, we adopted a ten-month-old girl who had a mental disability. When she first came to us, she had temper tantrums, and she would cry until she passed out. Her file was stamped "Unadoptable."

Others quickly followed. Most of the children had been abused physically, mentally, or emotionally, and their files were stamped unadoptable too. One of the girls whose legs were crippled by polio walked on her hands when she first came to us. Others struggled with crossed eyes, cerebral palsy, mental illness, and learning disabilities. Two of the children, ages three and one, had been marred by the unthinkable—since birth they had been used in the prostitution business.

One by one our family grew. We were multicultural long before anyone used that term. Our kids were Korean, Vietnamese, African, Puerto Rican, Native American, and Caucasian. When the older kids left for school in the morning, they never knew who might be added to the family by the time they got home. If there was one more kid added to the mix, everyone just moved their stuff around and made room.

While I was busy caring for our children, Henry worked as a minister and also created an outreach program to feed the poor. But the magnanimous public image he developed differed from his personality at home. When it came to our own family, Henry was starting to become domineering. I was hesitant to even ask for money to take the kids on a field trip or out for doughnuts. Finally, I gave up asking and made a decision to earn my own income. I started an in-home day care that I operated for twenty-nine years.

Still, I often wondered if I was deficient in judgment when it came to running a home or in other areas of my life. I sought advice from books on how to nurture our marriage. I signed the two of us up for relationship-building seminars at church that might help us understand each other.

Henry often pacified me by saying, "Things will get better." But they never did. Then he would tell me, "Most of the problems in this marriage are your fault, you know."

All I could do was mutter, "I'm sorry." As a child I had felt that I seldom measured up to my parents' expectations, so as a wife I was not surprised to be a disappointment.

With Henry's dominant attitude, his recurring bouts of poor health, and the resultant financial strain, our relationship crumbled. But I was raised with the belief that divorce was unacceptable in a Christian marriage. I relied on commitment to get me through each day.

I also gained strength from a decision that I made as a young girl. When I was nine, I attended a Good Friday service at my church. Near the end of the service the pastor gave a verbal invitation to all present. He spread out his arms and in a clear and tender voice said, "If you would like to give your life to Jesus Christ, please come to the altar."

I had sat through services like that many times before, but that day the minister's voice touched my heart. I wanted to feel loved the way the pastor talked about love. I wanted to be accepted the way Jesus accepted those who were scorned. I wanted unconditional love.

I went forward and prayed. I confessed my sins, sought God's forgiveness, and asked Him to help me make decisions. From that day on I read the Bible repeatedly to learn what God wanted me to do.

Through decades of a strained marriage, I relied on Jesus's power whenever life took a wild turn. But I could have never imagined how completely I would need to lean on Him in my darkest hour.

One night as I cleaned up the kitchen after supper I was startled by loud shouts and pounding on the front and the back door. "Open up! This is the police!" they shouted.

Henry opened the door. A half dozen burly officers pressed inside with their guns drawn. One of them read Henry and me our rights. The others corralled the eleven children under age eighteen and, in hushed tones, talked with them in the next room. Soon each child went to their bedroom and came back with a small bag of their things. Before I could make any sense out of what was happening, the policemen started taking the children out the door.

"What are you doing?" I sobbed. "What's going on? Where are you taking our kids?"

I couldn't comprehend what I was seeing. I stared at Henry, who looked as dumbfounded as I.

"How can this be?" I screamed. "You can't just *take* our children."

I hugged and kissed the little ones until officers pried them out of my arms. I tried to console the ones who didn't understand what was happening any more than I did. Then they were shepherded into waiting vans. An officer restrained me as I ran toward the door. The last I saw of my children were the taillights of those vans disappearing into the darkness.

After they were gone, the police told my husband he was under arrest. Then they asked me what seemed like dozens of questions. Sometimes the same question was asked three different ways. They kept pressing me for information until I thought they might arrest me too.

Finally, they told me why they had come: "Two of your daughters and one of your sons told their school counselor that their father has sexually abused them."

"That is not true!" I said. "I have spent years putting love and care into our home. This couldn't happen in our house without my knowing it." I turned to Henry. "What are they talking about?" I asked him. "How can they say these things?"

"I don't know," he said. "I just don't know."

But the officers took him away and left me there reeling in my nightmare. How can a mother scrub dishes at the kitchen sink one minute and have her children ripped from her life the next? "Jesus, Jesus, please watch over my children," I prayed over and over again. "Keep them safe."

Days passed without any answers. My phone calls to the agency and my desperate pleas for information were met with a generic response: "I'm sorry, Mrs. Grafs, we cannot give out any information."

Like Rachel of the Old Testament weeping for her little ones, I could not be comforted. My children were gone. While I entrusted each of my children to God, I clung to the desperate hope that they would all come home again—and that life would return to normal. But even if it didn't, I drew comfort from the knowledge that someday there would be a grand reunion in heaven. God is always good.

With Henry away, I spent many hours in thought and prayer. I was plagued with guilt and too embarrassed to confide in anyone. I knew I needed to keep an eternal perspective, but how could God still love me?

Again and again I repeated the first verses I had memorized as a child: "For God loved the world so much that he gave his only Son so that anyone [even me] who believes in him shall not perish but have eternal life" (John 3:16, TLB). I also looked to God's promises in the Old Testament: "They will not labor in vain, or bear children for calamity; for they are the offspring of those blessed by the LORD, and their descendants with them" (Isa. 65:23, NASU).

A few days later, Henry was finally released from jail. When he walked in the front door, I asked him what had happened. "They are crazy," he said. "They say I have molested our children. You *know* I haven't."

The children were interviewed again. This time the police presented a strong case against my husband. Eventually he admitted that he had done the terrible things they accused him of. I was full of remorse. My poor children—I had let them down.

I didn't want to show my face in public. What were our neighbors thinking? How could I explain to relatives what had happened? Every day for years, I prayed to die. My embarrassment and humiliation, though great, were nothing compared to the grief of losing my children. My precious family had been forever torn apart.

Somehow Henry avoided prosecution and a prison sentence. I don't know how. One of my older daughters who was married and living nearby asked why I had allowed her father back under our roof. "You can't even have your grandchildren visit if he's home," she said.

"I know," I replied. "I know." Only the commitment of my long-ago vows kept me from demanding that he leave. His health declined significantly, and I thought, "Where will he go in his old age? Who can he rely on?" So I took care of him until he died.

Jesus never promised that faith would exempt me from trials or hardship. And my faith did not insulate me from the wrenching in my heart when I wept for my children. I still grieve that they were hurt and that my family's relationships were broken by sin. But I rejoice that, for a while, God allowed me to wrap my arms around those who had been scorned by the meanness of the world. Even though that time was too brief, He allowed me to give unconditional love to those deemed unlovable.

Today I bask in frequent visits and phone calls from my children. "I love you, Mom," they say, and it is sweet music to my ears.

Through great trials, God strengthened my patience and gift of mercy. I look to the day of our family's grand reunion in heaven, and meanwhile the Lord continues to walk with me each new day. God is good—all the time.

Guiding Principles

A Pinch of Salt

> - Remember that all we own is a gift from God—a gift He can recall at any time.

> - Lean on God in your small struggles. That way, when great trials come, you will feel comfortable depending on Him. "We were under great pressure, far beyond our ability to endure, so that we despaired even of life. Indeed, in our hearts we felt the sentence of death. But this happened that we might not rely on ourselves but on God, who raises the dead" (2 Cor. 1:8–9).

> Search your Bible for comfort. Join a study group so others can pray for you and help you understand God's Word. "He will deliver us. On him we have set our hope that he will continue to deliver us, as you help us by your prayers" (2 Cor. 1:10–11).

> If you focus on the things of this earth, you will eventually be disappointed or hurt. Seek rather to learn God's will and to please *Him*. "But seek first His kingdom and His righteousness, and all these things will be added to you" (Matt. 6:33, NAS).

Homemade With Heart

One of Esther's Favorite Recipes

This recipe feeds a lot of people. How many servings it is, I am not sure. We never count at our house. Different kinds of rice require differing amounts of water, but with a little experimentation, you soon figure out the exact formula.

African Chow Mein

2 large onions, chopped
2 cups celery, chopped
1½ to 2 lbs. ground turkey or hamburger meat
1½ cups uncooked white rice (or a mixture of white and brown rice)
½ cup soy sauce
2 cans cream of chicken soup
2 cans cream of mushroom soup
2 cans water (use soup cans)
1 can sliced mushrooms

1 cup blanched almonds
1 can water chestnuts (optional)

In a small skillet, sauté onions and celery in butter. In another large skillet, brown ground turkey or hamburger meat.

Mix all the ingredients together and transfer to a casserole dish. Bake for 2 hours at 350°F (add more water if too dry).

Now for an Update

With a Cherry on Top

God still calls on Esther's nurturing instincts even though she is now seventy-seven years old. She likes to invite college girls for impromptu Sunday dinners after church, sharing whatever she has on hand that has been purchased from her limited budget. "It gives them a taste of home," she says. She also rejoices in precious time spent with her large, loving family.

He Gives and Takes Away

A conversation with Janis Hackman

The LORD gave me what I had, and the LORD has taken it
away. Praise the name of the LORD!

—JOB 1:21, NLT

Don and I dawdled over our coffee. We met for the first time earlier
that night at my church's praise service for singles. After chatting
together at length in the sanctuary, he asked me out for dessert. We
explored several topics and had some great laughs, and then our
conversation took on a more serious tone.

"I recently lost my wife of thirty-two years to cancer," he said. His
voice quivered and his head drooped as he told me.

"I can tell you still miss her," I said.

"I miss her so much, but she urged me repeatedly to marry again as
soon as I was ready." I did not respond, but I noticed the nervous tic
on his face. "I have been praying about what to do next," he said.

Don and I were attracted to one another from the start—I, a middle-
aged woman, and this tall, lanky man with graying hair, obvious
intelligence, and a deep sensitivity. The waitress refilled our coffee
cups several times as we proffered one topic after another. Before long
we were talking like old friends.

Then Don told me again how he had been asking God to guide
him to the right person to marry. "I didn't know how to pray about
it," Don said, "but my daughter reminded me to be specific. That is
difficult when you don't know which attributes the two of you need in
order to build a good marriage. So far I have concluded that I should
ask God to lead me to a woman in her late forties or early fifties who
has never been married before. She needs to be an on-fire Christian,

and it would be very nice if she were an elementary school teacher like me so we could have that in common."

I didn't know what to say, so I didn't say anything. I matched those criteria in every detail.

Don was a bit flustered by my silence. "Then last week," he blurted, "I sensed in my spirit I was to come to your church to meet my future wife. It makes me feel a bit foolish to tell you this, but it's the truth."

I went home that evening with much to ponder. For days, my thoughts alternated between warning messages that told me to be cautious and exhilarating daydreams about an exciting new life in store.

The next weekend I invited Don to come with me to church. He didn't know it, but a year before a Christian had prophesied over me and said, "You will marry a tall man in a brown coat." I accepted her words with skepticism, but when Don walked in that Sunday wearing a brown tweed jacket, I had to smile.

So the two of us became a couple. Don was a man of integrity, and I was reassured to discover that some of my relatives had known him for years. We talked on several occasions about his deceased wife and what their marriage had been like. He told me he trusted the Lord, not his emotions, concerning his future. He liked to write, and passionate love letters began to pour out of him. Gradually, I became convinced that Don loved me for myself and not merely as a replacement for his wife.

Four months after we met, Don and I celebrated with a church wedding, our families and friends in attendance. I moved into his lakeside home, and we asked his two daughters if they wanted to take their mother's things. They said they trusted us to pass her treasures along to them after we finished enjoying them. What a privilege to have won the favor of his children.

Our adjustment to married life went smoothly. Don and I were both financially conservative—I more so than he because I had always lived on the modest salary of a parochial school teacher.

Although I typically shopped for clothes at consignment stores, Don had other ideas about that. "Let's go out and buy you a dress at an upscale store," he would insist over my protests. We enjoyed ourselves as I tried on a few outfits and watched him smile. He loved buying nice things for me.

Both of us had tithed most of our lives. I heard about the concept of tithing when I was in high school, so when I got my first job, I decided to give 10 percent of my paycheck to the church. There was plenty of money left to meet my expenses, so I gradually increased the amount to 15 percent. I continued tithing all my adult life and always had food to eat, clothes to wear, and a place to live.

For the most part, I was content with what I had and was not tempted to spend more than I earned. Clearly, God was my provider, and even though I didn't earn a large salary, I never had to worry about finances. Now to have a husband who held similar beliefs to mine was an added blessing.

Don joined my church after we were married, and together we participated in various prayer ministries. He retired from his teaching position and started working on a book and writing for a local newspaper. We sold the house and downsized to a townhouse. For several years, life was good.

Then Don's health started to fail. Diabetes had plagued him for years, and he began to have problems with his heart. I would be folding clothes or making lunch and hear him call out, "Get me to the hospital!" Whatever I was doing had to wait. Over the next few months, we made many urgent trips to the doctor's office and the hospital with Don clutching his chest and gasping for breath.

"Hey, watch out," he said one day as we sped down the freeway. "The car ahead of us just turned and went up a hill." Comments like that were hard to ignore, but I came to realize that his oxygen-deprived brain was playing tricks on him.

"Everything is OK, Don. It's all right. We'll be there soon," I would reassure him.

But Don was not all right. After repeated emergency trips to the hospital, the doctor finally placed him on the waiting list for a heart transplant. The doctor also requested an LVAD (left ventricular assistance device) that could be surgically implanted to improve Don's blood circulation. FDA approval was still pending at that time, so LVADs were hard to get.

Meanwhile, Don endured many medical tests and delay after delay. At one point he was hospitalized for extensive testing to determine whether or not an LVAD would be sufficiently effective in his case. On day five of his hospital stay, we got word that the lab in another state had lost his blood samples. "Forget it, then!" Don said, and proceeded to check himself out of the hospital.

"If you don't stay on the list," the doctor advised, "you will have only a year, at the most, to live." But Don had had enough. He was tired. He knew his Savior and his eternal destination, and he wanted to quit the futile fight for longevity and enjoy the time he had left.

His doctor told him that since the medications were no longer of much benefit, he could taper off on taking them. Don weighed the decision carefully, but once it was made, he was at peace.

Overnight my life changed, and I plummeted into grief. Within months I would be alone again after nearly twenty years of marriage. From the beginning, Don had been in charge of our combined finances, and he had strong opinions. He avoided insurance policies because he was positive the Lord would return before he died. Neither of us was entitled to teacher's pensions; Don had not taught for the number of years required, and all of my experience was with small private schools. We did not have a savings account either.

Yet when I thought about it, I knew we had many assets. Our townhouse was paid for, and we didn't have any huge debt. If I needed more income, I could substitute teach at the elementary level because I had kept my license current.

Don got sicker, and life got harder. The tall prince who had wooed me with love letters was losing his pleasant personality to overwhelming health issues. Hospice workers came to the house at all hours to check on him, but Don was weak, exhausted, and uncomfortable, and that made him short-tempered. In his pain and frustration, he would make harsh comments that made me cringe.

I began to fall apart. I started sleeping in the guest bedroom so I could get more rest. I also made the decision to see a Christian counselor even though I had always heard, "People who go to shrinks don't have enough faith." The counseling helped me cope with my fears and gain a better perspective on what was happening and my reaction to it.

Several women in my church showed extra concern for me during that time, and it helped tremendously. Some of them were widows already familiar with the heartache that now plagued me. During those months, I memorized Psalm 91 and repeated it often.

> He who dwells in the shelter of the Most High will rest in the shadow of the Almighty. I will say of the LORD, "He is my refuge and my fortress, my God, in whom I trust." Surely he will save you from the fowler's snare and from the deadly pestilence. He will cover you with his feathers, and under his wings you will find refuge; his faithfulness will be your shield and rampart. You will not fear the terror of night, nor the arrow that flies by day, nor the pestilence that stalks in the darkness, nor the plague that destroys at midday.... "Because he loves me," says the LORD, "I will rescue him; I will protect him, for he acknowledges my name. He will call upon me, and I will answer him; I will be with him in trouble, I will deliver him and honor him. With long life will I satisfy him and show him my salvation."
>
> —PSALM 91:1–6, 14–16

Near the end of Don's life, God did a miracle for us. One Saturday morning, I went to a women's prayer gathering at church and lingered afterward to pray at the altar. I knelt and tears flooded my eyes. Don had only a short time to live, and yet our relationship festered like an open wound. I did not want things to end this way.

Someone tapped me on the shoulder, and I turned to see Tom, a friend of Don's, standing there. "I've been meeting with a prayer partner down the hall," he said, "and the Lord sent me here to tell you He has seen your distress." He then asked if I would join him and his friend for a few minutes.

We went down the hall to a lounge area often used by small groups. "We sensed during our prayer time that Don is very ill and has been taking it out on you," the other man said. I had kept that particular problem a secret, so it wasn't possible that they could have known unless the Lord told them. As they gently questioned me, I confirmed that what they sensed was true.

Tom called a few days afterward and made arrangements to talk with Don. Later that evening, after Tom had left, I heard a knock at my bedroom door. "Can I talk with you for a minute?" Don asked as he poked his head through my open door, his gaunt body leaning against its frame. "I want to ask your forgiveness for being so nasty these past few weeks. I couldn't seem to help myself, but I know that is no excuse. I want things to be good between us again."

With that, the sweetness between us returned. I could sense God's peace again, and I knew Don was experiencing it too. A few days later, God took him home.

The grace and timing of Don's death serves as a poignant reminder that God is in control and all we have to do is trust Him. I knew when the Lord brought us together over coffee eighteen years earlier that I was about to experience His provision in new and exciting ways. That never changed, even during the time Don was ill. Because the Lord is my strength, my refuge, and my fortress, I can look to the future without worry. I can smile at the future with hope.

Guiding Principles

A Pinch of Salt

> Realize that the most powerful emotion you might feel as a new widow is relief. When a death is gradual, the survivor often begins grieving ahead of time. The book titled *Dying With Grace* by Judson Cornwall can help you keep things in proper perspective.[2]

> Use the services of hospice care if appropriate for your situation. Hospice workers are wonderful not only for providing expert physical care, but also for giving counsel and solace to caregivers. They even offer activities designed to bring healing after your loved one's death.

> Avoid pity parties by refusing to dwell on negative thoughts. Trust God instead. You might want to memorize this verse: "We demolish arguments and every pretension that sets itself up against the knowledge of God, and we take captive every thought to make it obedient to Christ" (2 Cor. 10:5).

> Let your grief make you more empathetic toward others, especially other widows. Reach out and help someone. Perhaps the book *The Friendships of Women* by Dee Brestin can be of help.[3]

> Maintain a healthy lifestyle, and take good care of yourself. Eat well and exercise daily even if you find

it difficult to stay motivated. Remember, your body is what will get you around for many years to come.

Homemade With Heart

One of Janis's Favorite Recipes

I got this recipe from Elizabeth Hopkins at the Black Hills Health and Education Center in Hermosa, South Dakota. Don and I spent three weeks there in 2003 learning some of the specifics on how to lead healthier lives.

Good-for-You Granola

20 cups rolled oats
2 cups sunflower seeds
2 cups white sesame seeds
2 cups almonds, slivered or whole
3 cups water
1 cup olive oil
1 cup pineapple juice (or use apple juice concentrate, sucanat [unrefined cane sugar], or unsweetened shredded coconut)
Raisins or craisins (dried cranberries)

Mix the oats, sunflower seeds, sesame seeds, and almonds together in a very large bowl. In a medium-sized bowl, combine the water, olive oil, and pineapple juice. Pour the liquid mixture over the oats mixture. Stir until well blended.

Spray four shallow pans (cookie sheets, 9 x 13 inch cake pans, etc.) with olive oil. Divide the granola evenly between the pans. Bake uncovered at 225°F for 8 hours. Your house will smell so good when it's done.

After the granola cools, add the plumped raisins or craisins. Store in ziplock plastic bags or in a large, tightly covered container.

Now for an Update

With a Cherry on Top

After her husband's death, Janis enrolled in a Crown Financial Ministries course at her church in order to get a better handle on her finances. One of her first assignments was to list her assets along with her liabilities. The research made her realize how much God had already provided for her, and a year after taking the Crown course, she was debt free. She said, "I was a queen sitting in a castle, and I didn't know."

Six

Flavor With Love

BE MY VALENTINE!" A SWEET SENTIMENT FOR SURE, BUT NOT for everyone. Whether the single life or remarriage is in your future is a matter of individual preference and God's plan. But the final decision is far beyond the simplicity of a heart-shaped confection or a cookie-cutter romance.

Amy Bishop was not looking for love in the wrong places, or even in the *right* places, so when God put someone in her path, she was more than a bit surprised. Read how Amy learned to trust God's ways when He told her to be still.

Marriage was not in author Sharon Knudson's forecast either, but when she sought wise counsel and then took a dare, she came to a different conclusion. "Those Cherry Macaroons" is a story about how cookies played a role in blessing not only her but also a bachelor.

After her little girl begged Aubrey Claxton for a "forever family," Aubrey complained to God that the demise of her marriage was unfair. Because she was concentrating so hard on earning a living, she was not expecting what the God of second chances had in store.

Whether God gives us a special love or fulfills us in our single life, He is the provider of all love. Familial love is that special bond between family and friends. Romantic love speaks of sexual intimacy in marriage. But agape love surpasses them both. It is the unconditional love relationship between God and humankind.

Be Still

A conversation with Amy Bishop

This is what the Sovereign LORD, the Holy One of Israel, says: "In repentance and rest is your salvation, in quietness and trust is your strength."

—ISAIAH 30:15

"John, do you take Amy to be your wife?"

"I do."

Oh, how I loved that deep voice! How I loved his booming laugh. How I loved this man.

I had already been married twice. The first and second marriages were to the same man. I tried hard to honor my vows, but my husband was so abusive that I was lucky to escape the relationship alive.

Our nine-year-old son made me realize how desperate my situation was when I sat at the edge of his bed one evening to say good night. I leaned over to kiss him on the forehead and then added an extra blanket to keep him warm. As I tucked it in around him, I felt hard lumps beneath my fingers. I flipped the covers back and gasped at what I saw. There beside him lay two butcher knives!

"What on earth?" I gasped.

Wide-eyed, Zachariah said, "I know Dad hurts you. The next time you scream, I'm going to kill him."

I took my son and left the next morning.

"Amy, do you take John to be your husband?"

"I do."

Finally my life had taken a positive turn. Before I met John, I had sworn off all men. Zachariah and I had settled into a quiet routine of school, work, and church life. I had grown up with a strong faith and felt comfortable in God's love. I didn't always understand His ways or know why He allowed certain things to happen, but I believed that if I honored Him, He would bless my life. And John was a blessing—an unexpected blessing.

Neither he nor I had been looking for a mate. My father had recently begun a food ministry that fed hundreds of people a week. I volunteered to help and met many wonderful workers. One of them was John, a man who laughed with his whole body—a big, booming laugh. He had a smile that made me want to smile right back.

He was handy too, and Dad said, "John might enjoy fixing stuff for you at the house."

"I guess that would be OK," I said, knowing I could use the help.

Soon John and I became good friends. I felt comfortable when I asked him to repair broken furniture or tend to electrical problems. After a few months, he started lingering when the work was finished, and we would eat supper, watch a movie, or go shopping together.

One night as we walked through the aisles of our local home-improvement store, John said, "May I hold your hand?"

No man had ever asked permission to touch me. "He is such a gentleman," I thought. I felt as if he handed me an armful of roses and placed a tiara on my head.

A month later we were watching a movie when John asked if he could give me a kiss. I was astounded. No one had ever treated me with such respect. That first kiss was in February, and we were married in July. It was a God-given marriage. John treated me like a queen, making me feel special and beautiful. And he loved my son. Zachariah was a young man by then, and he loved John too.

As wonderful as John was, he was not perfect. He liked to drink. I didn't say anything at first, but as the frequency and amount increased, I wanted to talk to him about it. I hoped a loving approach would make a difference.

As I prayed about the drinking, I sensed God affirming this calm approach. Again and again I seemed to hear, "Be still, and know that I am God" (Ps. 46:10).

Impatience set in, but still I obeyed and kept my mouth shut. I was tempted to nag him, but somehow I knew that attitude would only make things worse. So I kept quiet.

John continued to drink, and it made him ornery. One night at a local retail store, he got into an argument with a cashier. He was being too boisterous, and she called for store security. When John wouldn't leave, the police were notified, and he was arrested. I didn't know anything about it until he called me and said, "Honey, I'm in the detox unit."

"What!" I said, trying to remember God's directive to "be still." I was both angry and relieved—angry that he had been drinking, but also relieved that he was forced to come face-to-face with his addiction.

"What happens now?" I asked. "How long will they keep you?"

"I don't know," he answered. "Maybe they will tell me tomorrow."

A few days later, John stood before a judge who sentenced him to inpatient treatment for alcohol abuse. I drove home from the hearing and thought about what had just happened. I wondered what lay ahead. Would the time away strengthen his resolve to give up alcohol, or would he continue to drink?

I walked into the empty house that day and knew I had to pray. I sat on the couch and picked up my devotional. I opened it to that day's reading. "Be still, and know that I am God..." it read. I took it as a confirmation of what God had been telling me all along.

Once the inpatient care was finished, John told me he would have fought any attempt I might have made to do an intervention. I smiled. God's "be still" directive was exactly right. I had my sweet John back, and his drinking was never a problem again. He was my best friend, and I was his.

One night around 9:30, John dropped me off at the group home where I worked as a program counselor with mentally and physically challenged adults. At about 2:00 a.m., he called and said, "I just wanted to tell you that I love you dearly. I will be there to pick you up at six."

"I love you too," I told him. I went back to my duties.

When 6:00 a.m. rolled around, I was not surprised that John didn't arrive on time because seven inches of new snow had fallen during the night. When he still had not picked me up at six-thirty, I called home, but there was no answer.

I waited a little longer, thinking he was on his way. When he didn't show up by seven o'clock, I ran out of patience. My supervisor said I could use the company van if I brought it back within a couple of hours. So I got in the company van and turned on the wipers to clear the windshield. They thump-bumped in the quiet of the morning. Thick snow padded the streets and parks, and the peace contrasted my irritation with John.

I fumed all the way home because he hadn't kept his promise. "How can he call me and talk all lovey-dovey," I fumed, "and then not show up to get me?"

When I got to our house I saw the car parked on the street—a shapeless blob under the snow. John had made no attempt to even shovel it out. I stopped and got out of the van, slammed the door extra hard, and stomped into the house. There sat John in his rocking chair!

"John Thomas Bishop, what is your problem?" I yelled while I tugged off my boots. Then I stomped across the living room, huffing as I passed John and ran into the bathroom.

Then I heard a thud. What was that? What could make that kind of noise? I looked around the corner.

"John!" I screamed. My three-hundred-fifty-pound husband had fallen out of his rocking chair. Now he lay sprawled and unconscious on the living room rug.

Being a medical assistant, I started CPR. I also made a quick call for emergency help, then went back to doing chest compressions and resuscitations, "One-and, two-and, three-and…"

"Come on, baby, come on," I said over and over. "Please don't leave me." I prayed that the ambulance would get there quickly. Then I heard the sirens.

"They're coming, John…hang on, honey…they're getting closer…" I kept saying to him.

The paramedics rushed into the house. They worked on John as furiously as I had, and they checked his vital signs. John's chest didn't move. His eyelids never fluttered. His skin looked ashy and felt cool. They worked on him for almost an hour before they slid him into the ambulance. "You can ride along in the front," the attendant told me.

We sped down the street as the sirens cleared traffic. Bundled-up kids looked up from the snowmen they were building in their front yards. "How can everything look so bright and sparkly when John is fighting for his life?" I wondered. Intellectually, I knew John was dead, but my heart didn't get the message.

"Please, God, don't take John," I prayed.

When we arrived at the hospital, the paramedics rushed John into the emergency room where the doctors and nurses crowded around him. Within just a few minutes, the attending physician's words forced me to face what I already knew. "I'm sorry," the doctor told me. "There was nothing more we could do. Your husband died of natural causes—probably two or three hours ago."

"Just a few hours after he called me," I thought. Then I burst into tears. Did John somehow know he was going to die? In the days that followed, I kept thinking back to that final phone call. I was so thankful for those last words: "I just wanted to tell you that I love you dearly."

I got through the funeral, but I was angry with God for taking John. I just couldn't imagine life without my companion. Our seven years together had been too short. I had to know why God took my blessing away.

Days and weeks dragged as if I lived on a slow-motion roller coaster. Some days I was at the top and could see my way clearly. But mostly, I was at the bottom, inching my way along. My neglected Bible and devotional books beckoned from the table. I tried to pray, but I couldn't concentrate. All the fun John had brought to my life ground to a halt. Then one day, I heard the Lord say, "Praise Me."

"I don't want to," was my reply.

"Praise Me," He said again.

I couldn't. I missed John too much. I missed his smell, I missed his hugs, and I missed his big, booming laugh. If only I could hear that hardy roar one more time. "Why, God, why?" I asked Him continually. But God was patient with me even as I kept a tight grip on my grudge.

Angry or not, and maybe out of habit, I continued to attend church. One morning the pastor asked me a question that led to a change of heart. "We need an additional worship leader," he said. "Will you consider the job?"

I have always loved music, and John and I often sang together around the house. I did not want to disappoint the pastor, and I knew our congregation needed someone to fill the position. "Yes," I answered him. "When do you want me to start?"

"As soon as you are ready," the pastor said.

I didn't feel ready, and I didn't know if I would ever be ready. But I stepped out in faith. Each week as I prepared for Sunday worship, my enthusiasm grew. The old hymns I loved seeped into my bones and penetrated my heart. They played in my mind, and I hummed them as I worked around the house. My attitude toward God softened and allowed Him to heal me from the inside out. I smiled more.

One day a neighbor stopped by and said, "Forgive me for asking, but every night I see two big men standing at your doors. One stands at the front and one at the back. I watch for a long time, but I never see them leave. Who are they?"

"They must be my angels," I answered. Even though I had never seen the two men myself, I knew God had sent them to watch over me. I felt John's love, and I felt God's love.   .

With hymns in my heart, angels at the doors, and the passage of time, I was able to let go of John. Not right away, but the ache eased enough over the next two years that I was able to see the blessings God continued to send.

I set out on new adventures. One of those involved my mother who had recently become a widow too. She had been married for fifty-three years, spending most of the last fifteen years caring for my father. Together we answered a call for a short-term mission trip to Africa. We spent fourteen days with families who rejoiced in God's Word and who hungered for more. Both of us know we are supposed to go back to Africa to serve long term, so we are just waiting to hear from God for His timing.

I love to tell people about God's promises, especially His promise of eternal life and being reunited with our loved ones. I know I will see John again someday. I will see his smile beam at me the minute I set foot in heaven. And when John sees me, he will scoop me up in his big arms, and his whole body will laugh—a big, booming laugh.

Guiding Principles

A Pinch of Salt

> Praise Him even when you don't feel like it! Keep a song in your heart and music in your soul. Whether it's an old hymn, a modern song of praise, or an upbeat instrumental, let it soothe your spirit.

> Keep your heart and your mind open to God. Count on the promises of His blessings.

> Remember that there are many wonderful, tender men in the world. You never know if God will bring one of them to you when you least expect it. Remain open to God's plan if He does bring a new man into your life.

> God is patient. Take time to heal, and then answer His call. Be ready to meet the needs of people in your neighborhood or congregation, and do not be surprised if God uses you for His kingdom in mighty ways you never dreamed of!

> Try not to be impatient with God. Study His Word to find out what is pleasing to Him.

> Strive to "be still" and obey.

Homemade With Heart

One of Amy's Favorite Recipes

Crazy Chocolate Cake was passed down in our family from my maternal grandmother, whom we fondly called Nanny. The recipe was popular during the Great Depression because it does not require eggs. My sister Annie made it for John and me on our wedding day. It has been a favorite for generations!

Crazy Chocolate Cake

3 cups flour
2 tsp. baking soda
2 cups sugar
1 tsp. salt

⅓ cup cocoa powder
1 tsp. vanilla
2 Tbsp. white vinegar
¾ cup vegetable oil
2 cups cold water

Mix all ingredients together by hand in a large bowl.

Bake in a greased, 9 x 13 inch pan for 35–45 minutes at 350°F.

Best Chocolate Frosting Ever

2 cups white sugar
½ cup butter
½ cup cocoa powder
½ cup milk
1 tsp. vanilla

Stir all ingredients together in a nonstick kettle. Bring to a full, rolling boil and remove from heat. Cool thoroughly and stir until it reaches the right thickness to spread (it will finish hardening as it sits on the cake).

Now for an Update

With a Cherry on Top

Amy and her widowed mother live together, and during two weeks of every summer, they have joined forces to create a special, fun-filled week at her house for their grandchildren and great-grandchildren. That's when they run Grandma Camp. The kids are with them twenty-four hours a day, seven days a week. (The only requirement is that the children must be potty trained!)

The grandmas set up a tent and a quality blowup swimming pool next to their bountiful garden. Daily activities include picking berries and making jam, decorating t-shirts, going on field trips, and cooking supper. One of the kids' favorite treats is going out to a restaurant to eat—somewhere other than a fast-food chain. This is a great opportunity to reinforce dressing up and using proper table manners. The grandmas, ever mindful of God's directives to teach, assign the children Bible verses to memorize: "Train up a child in the way he should go, even when he is old he will not depart from it" (Prov. 22:6, NASU). And "Do not provoke your children to anger, but bring them up in the discipline and instruction of the Lord" (Eph. 6:4, NASU).

Those Cherry Macaroons

A conversation with Sharon

> You protect me from the power of death. I have served you faithfully, and you will not abandon me to the world of the dead. You will show me the path that leads to life; your presence fills me with joy and brings me pleasure forever.
> —PSALM 16:10–11, GNT

I stirred the dough for a batch of cookies, taking a moment to savor the delicious aroma of almond flavoring. I nibbled on a few flakes of coconut as I chopped the walnuts and maraschino cherries, the whole time remembering how nervous I had been when I made this special recipe so many years ago.

That summer I attended a weeklong Christian retreat in Colorado Springs. I diligently saved money for a year so I could have a vacation—my first time off since the divorce. I worked four jobs while enduring repeated sinus infections. I was in desperate need of a getaway.

The retreat center was nestled in the foothills of the Colorado mountains. Expansive acreage, towering trees, and a castle moat surrounded quaint stone buildings. Red rock formations unlike anything at home lifted my outlook from its habitual tiredness. What I enjoyed best, though, were the messages given by Pastor Bruce Wilkinson, who was the featured speaker each evening. His words found a home in my hurting heart and reminded me that God is love.

All week my weariness soaked in the teaching. After the final session Friday night, I approached Pastor Wilkinson to thank him. We chatted for a while, and he told me that, even though we had not previously spoken to each other, he had noticed the grief and heaviness I carried around. "Is there any way I can help you?" he asked. "Tell me what is happening in your life."

We each pulled up a chair, and I gave him the condensed version. My thirty-year marriage had ended two years before and I could not get over the loss. For one thing, I was working too hard at furnishing room and board to foreign students, managing a busy office at a Christian college, and acting as both organist and choir director at a nearby church. The combination gave me just enough income to meet expenses and keep my modest home.

I knew I was in trouble—physically rundown and close to burnout. I had been sick off and on for months, and, perhaps even worse, I had a bad case of self-pity that I could not seem to shake.

Pastor Wilkinson listened and nodded sympathetically. By then, only a few people remained at the back of the room, chatting in groups of two or three. He bowed his head and asked God to heal my grief and make me physically strong.

Then he looked at me and abruptly changed his tone. "Imagine there is a big book laying open on your lap," he said in an animated voice. "You have just finished a long, complicated chapter in your life. It's over! And now it's time to turn the page."

I balked mentally for a few moments, and then I realized he was right. Dutifully I imagined a big, heavy book laying open across my lap. Slowly and bravely, I mentally turned the page.

"What do you see in your future?" Pastor Wilkinson asked. "And *who* is in that next chapter?"

What I had envisioned for my future was work, work, and more work. I figured I would be eighty-two years old before I was financially sound. As for *who*, there was no who!

"Could there be a man who wants to come into your life?" he asked.

I was repulsed at the very thought. There was no man. I never, ever wanted to get married again. Ever!

I hesitated, speechless. Pastor Wilkinson waited silently.

"Are you *sure* there isn't a man in that chapter?" he asked again.

"Well," I finally said, "there is this one man in the church where I'm the organist, but I certainly have no romantic feelings toward him." My face burned hot, and it had no doubt turned a fiery red.

The man I was referring to was Bob, a quiet bachelor in his fifties. Bob was known for his integrity and kindness. He had been president of the congregation for many years. While I found it easy to discuss church business with him, there was never any hint of personal interest—only occasional sideways glances across the congregation on Sunday mornings.

"Does Bob have a good reputation?" Pastor Wilkinson inquired. "Do you wonder why he never married?"

This line of questioning was embarrassing, but he was relentless.

"Well, what do you think?" the pastor asked with finality. He was probably losing his patience with me a little.

"I don't know," I replied. New possibilities were racing through my thoughts. "But...probably...I *could* bless his life."

I could not believe what I had just said. Pastor Wilkinson grinned and sat back in his chair, folding his arms across his chest. "There you have it," he confirmed. "Maybe God has something in store for the two of you."

"I'm not looking for a man," I quickly reminded him. "I have no intention of pursuing anyone or marrying again."

"This is what I think you should do," the pastor said. "Go home and bake a batch of cookies. Put some on a nice plate—not a paper plate, but one that must be returned. Give them to Bob next Sunday and say, 'I baked some cookies and thought you might like some.' But be sure you don't say, 'I baked these cookies *for you*,' or anything like that."

I could not imagine doing something so outrageous.

"You said Bob is a bachelor," Pastor Wilkinson explained. "There is nothing more appealing to a bachelor than something homemade. Yet, there is no manipulation in this plan. Bob can eat those cookies and merely return the plate. Or, if he likes, he can take a step toward you. Either way, you have opened the door just a crack. Things could proceed or they could abruptly end; it will be up to Bob. Your job, Sharon, will be to pray for God's will and promise that you will be content with whatever Bob decides."

I was still trying to evaluate such a preposterous plan, but the pastor fidgeted in his chair as if he was ready to leave. "You think about it," he said. "Why don't we pray once more before we go." I bowed my head and closed my eyes.

"Lord!" Pastor Wilkinson's voice was loud, and it startled me; I jumped. "Give Bob to Sharon!" he declared. Then he paused before adding, "And give Sharon to Bob!"

He closed his prayer a few words later, and then gave me an impish smile as he said, "Send me your wedding invitation, OK?"

"This is too much," I thought. I could not believe his audacity. In a way, I wanted to slug him. But in another way, I was thankful that he gave me something to consider, even if it was audacious.

The retreat ended, and I flew home the next morning. By Saturday evening, I was wondering whether or not I should bake those cookies.

I could not get those words out of my mind: "I baked some cookies and thought you might like some." I thought the idea was foolish, yet it might be the perfect thing.

Late that night, I paged through some recipe books. *If* I baked cookies (and that was still debatable), what kind would I make? It would have to be something special, not an ordinary, everyday cookie. And it would have to be hearty enough for a man. There, I found it—cherry macaroons!

I was tired but decided I had better get it over with. I checked the cupboards, and all the necessary ingredients were there. Before long the cookies were measured and stirred, dolloped and baked, and set to cool on the counter. I chose an antique plate from the hutch—a pink one to match the cookies—and I hastily arranged a dozen to make a mound. I covered them with plastic and slid them inside a brown paper bag to take to church the next day.

Throughout the morning, the camouflaged cookies sat next to me on the front pew and toyed with my concentration. I was the worship leader and I found it almost impossible to do my job. "Oh, Lord, have I done the right thing?" I prayed, "I want Your will for my life. Don't let me mess things up."

After the service, after the much-too-lengthy coffee hour, after nearly everyone had filtered out of the church, Bob returned to the sanctuary to close the windows and doors. Shaking so much I could hardly walk, I followed him in, thrust the bag of cookies at him, and blurted out, "Ibakedsomecookiesandthoughtyoumightlikesome!"

Then, overcome with embarrassment, I turned away, fled down the hall, down the steps, and out the front door to my car. All the way home I bawled, "How could I have humiliated myself like that? What on earth must the poor man be thinking?"

Days passed; no word from Bob.

On Friday night, he called. He mentioned that he had been weeding the marigolds in his garden. "My goodness," I thought to myself. "Here is a man who likes flowers."

"Thanks for the delicious cookies," Bob said after more small talk. "I'll return the plate to you on Sunday. Uh...would you like to go for lunch afterward, if...if you're not busy?"

There it was. Just as Pastor Wilkinson had said, Bob's hand was on the door I had so slightly cracked open. Now he was opening it farther, and to my surprise, I felt a surge of relief. In fact, I felt fine!

A year later, Bob and I were married. That little church was packed with our delighted family and friends. Since then I have repeatedly thanked God for the *gift* Bob has been to me. Many times, I have likened our love and marriage to a brand-new chapter in a great big book.

The kitchen timer rings, and my focus returns to the task at hand. When I switch the oven light on, I see the cookies are a healthy pink with light brown peaks. Glistening red cherries are poking through, and bakery smells fill the house.

"I made our favorite cookies again," I call out to Bob. "Come and have some cherry macaroons."

Guiding Principles

A Pinch of Salt

> Grieve the loss of your previous marriage fully, but do not be inconsolable. Allow yourself to move on when the time is right.

> Do not chase after a mate! "Those who rush to other gods bring many troubles on themselves" (Ps. 16:4, GNT). When we prioritize anything or any person over

God, they become "other gods" in our lives. Lead a life of purity so God can pour out His blessings on you.

> ▸ Immerse yourself in Scripture and find your comfort there. "You, Lord, are all I have, and you give me all I need; my future is in your hands. How wonderful are your gifts to me; how good they are! I praise the Lord, because he guides me, and in the night my conscience warns me. I am always aware of the Lord's presence; he is near, and nothing can shake me. And so I am thankful and glad, and I feel completely secure" (Ps. 16:5–9, GNT). These words were my motto, and during the years I was single, I slept with my Bible at night.

> ▸ Evaluate carefully any guidance offered by well-meaning people, especially if they speak with an uncanny authority. Unfortunately, there are manipulators who prey on those who are weak, broken, and vulnerable. There also are well-intentioned friends and relatives who express strong opinions in their attempts to intimidate or control. Do not blindly accept whatever someone proclaims, and do not accept advice without first praying earnestly and comparing what is said to the truths found in Scripture.

> ▸ Be open to God's leading, and obey Him whenever His directives are clear. Never say, "Never!" to God. "Trust in the LORD with all your heart; do not depend on your own understanding. Seek his will in all you do, and he will show you which path to take" (Prov. 3:5–6, NLT).

> ▸ Express your love and gratitude often to the Lord. Whether you remain on your own or one day marry, first and foremost, you are the beloved bride of Christ. Trust God's plan for your life, and be faithful to Him.

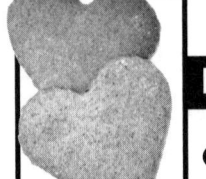

Homemade With Heart

One of Sharon's Favorite Recipes

The recipe for cherry macaroons was not new to me. I would some-times make them for my two daughters on Valentine's Day. Now the cookies are associated with the beginnings of Bob's and my romance. Many of our friends know the story of how we got together. Once in a while I will tease Bob, who thought he would forever be a bachelor, and say, "See what happened because you ate those cookies?"

Cherry Macaroon Cookies

½ cup butter
½ cup shortening
1 cup sugar
2 eggs
1¼ tsp. pure almond extract
2½ cups flour
1 tsp. baking powder
1 tsp. salt
¾ cup maraschino cherries, drained and diced
2 cups sweetened shredded or flaked coconut
1 cup nuts, coarsely chopped (use almonds, walnuts, pecans, or
    macadamia nuts)

Cream together butter and shortening. Gradually add sugar, eggs, and almond extract. Cream well. Blend in flour, baking powder, and salt. Add maraschino cherries, coconut, and nuts.

Drop by rounded spoonfuls onto lightly greased baking sheets. Bake 12–15 minutes at 350°F until lightly browned. Makes 5–6 dozen.

White Frosting (optional)

1 cup white chocolate chips
1 Tbsp. vegetable oil

Transfer cooled cookies to waxed paper or a baking rack. Combine white chocolate chips and oil, and place in microwave on high, stirring every 15 seconds until melted. Drizzle frosting over the cookies using a back-and-forth motion. Let frosting harden before storing.

Now for an Update

With a Cherry on Top

Bob and Sharon have already been married for more than a decade, and both are quick to thank God for their compatible partnership. Sharon is now a full-time speaker and freelance writer with hundreds of published articles and several books. In fact, "Those Cherry Macaroons" was the impetus for the *Starting From Scratch When You're Single Again* book. Visit Sharon's Web site at www.sharonknudson .com and rejoice with her in what God has done.

The God of Second Chances

A conversation with Aubrey Claxton

> He is...the God who gives life to the dead and calls things
> that are not as though they were.
>
> —ROMANS 4:17

I stared at the kitchen table in shocked disbelief. The innocuous-looking business envelope resting on its smooth maple surface held two hundred dollars in cash and the news that would change my life: my husband of three and a half years was gone!

He had written a resignation letter to the church where he was a youth minister and a note informing me that he was resigning our marriage and abdicating his duties as the daddy of our sixteen-month-old daughter. He also took the car and cleaned out our savings and checking accounts. On that cold, dark, February day, the only part I was missing was the explanation. It was not until after many months and a Nancy Drew–like investigation of my own that I found out he had left us to pursue a homosexual lifestyle.

My Sunday school class rallied around, packing and loading a moving van. I alternately threw things in anger, told my friends to take anything they wanted, and sat dully staring into space. My parents made a frantic long drive to the apartment where we were living. Ironically, that was to have been a temporary place while my husband and I shopped for a home. Within twenty-four hours, they had my daughter, Maggie, and me moved into my childhood home.

Two days later, I was served divorce papers via certified mail. And I was sure that my wrenching sobs were heard all over the city. It was the death of a marriage and the dreams I had dreamed since I was a little girl.

Oh, I know, statistically 50 percent of marriages—even Christian ones—end in divorce. It just was not part of *my* plan. Although our marriage certainly had its struggles, as all marriages do, mine had deeper issues than my naïveté, my idealism, or my optimism could begin to fathom. I ignored my growing isolation and the increasing incidents of him yelling at me or leaving for extended hours with no explanation. I put it down to the stress of our recent out-of-state move, having a baby, and the demands of ministry.

Maggie and I lived with my parents for six months until I secured a teaching position back in the town of our courtship. We moved and lived another six weeks with my aunt and uncle while we searched for a decent place to rent. And we lived that same six weeks on the humiliation of food stamps; my first paycheck didn't come until after mid-October. I taught all day, played with Maggie in the afternoons, searched for suitable housing in the evenings and on weekends, and fell exhausted into bed each night only to find that stress and worry would not allow me to sleep. Those were low days indeed.

Then one beautiful October day, a newspaper ad offered a glimmer of hope: a charming, if older, home in an OK neighborhood was for rent. It was clean, and the owners were Christians. They were willing to spray for spiders and have the carpets cleaned. In return, all they wanted were tenants who would not throw wild parties. (Their last renters had been a group of college students.) I assured them that Maggie and I were not the partying type.

Best of all, it had a red door, my very favorite color. As Maggie and I stood there, she spontaneously jumped up and down, clapping her hands. "Yea, God!" she exclaimed. "Our very own house with a red door!"

After Maggie reached two years of age, she began asking, "Why don't I have a daddy who comes home every night for dinner?" I struggled to find answers for that and other hard questions. I explained to her about poor choices that people sometimes make that regrettably affect others.

"OK," she chirped sweetly. "Then I want a baby brother or sister."

I sighed. "No, Maggie, it doesn't work that way. God gives babies to married people."

She was undeterred and continued with, "Who can marry us?" I can still hear the lilt in her voice and see the determination on her sweet little face as I explained the whole dating process. She wore me out, pestering me and praying every night about a "forever family."

I lived a very different life then, with different, self-imposed rules: no crying until after ten o'clock; no letting anyone close to me; only concentrating on Maggie, God, and finishing my master's degree to better provide for us. But still I wrestled with bitterness when I had to sell my wedding dress and wedding rings to pay the utility bills. I choked on resentment when my baby girl begged me not to go to work and to stay home with her instead. I pointed out to God that since I had saved myself for marriage and done things the right way, this was unfair treatment!

I pored over my Bible, threw myself on my knees in prayer, and journaled like crazy. Sometimes I was just tired. Other times I felt a loneliness that would have been impossible to explain to anyone else. I was so, so grateful for little Maggie.

One of the worst nights I remember came that first November. Maggie had a bad case of croup. I called the pediatrician and followed his orders. I stayed up all night, alternately standing under the shower spray, holding her in its steam, and walking out on the porch so she could breathe in the sharp, cold air. I held her and sobbed quietly, knowing that I would have to go to work the next morning, exhausted and worried about her. I didn't have a single sick day coming. "How will I ever do this alone," I wondered.

Even with wonderful support from my parents, for a single mom, issues of energy and money are constant struggles. Still I saw how God provided. During a particularly bitter winter, our utility bills were horrid. I did not say a word to anyone, but one Sunday the elders gave me an envelope with seventy-five dollars cash in it. With great compassion and tenderness, they urged, "Go to the grocery right now and buy some wonderful fresh fruit and some treats for you and that baby." Those *lights* during the blackout of this trial fueled my faith into brighter flames.

On those dark nights of my three and a half years of single parenting, I clung to God's promises. "For your Maker is your husband—the LORD Almighty is his name" (Isa. 54:5). I had decided it would probably be just Maggie and me for the rest of my life, and that would be fine. But God in His infinite goodness had other wonderful plans.

The most handsome police detective on the force was assigned to work juvenile crimes at the high school where I taught. He was a guest speaker who was witty and fascinating when my class was learning about constitutional law, the Fourth Amendment, and search and seizure. Then he began working security for the high school dances and often visited my room. My students began teasing me and caught on to Eli's interest even before I did.

For our first date, he bought me orange earplugs! We went to the firing range and then out for frozen custard. Our courtship was indeed a whirlwind. Our endless talks and my observations confirmed that he was a man of integrity and good character.

Eli also loved and accepted my daughter. On the day he presented me with a diamond solitaire engagement ring, he also gave engagement bracelets to my little girl. She went around telling everyone, "My mommy and me are getting married!"

Three months after saying a resounding "Yes!" to Eli's proposal, I was walked down the aisle by Maggie and my dad. During part of the ceremony, Eli repeated special family vows to Maggie that he had written himself. The closing song at our wedding was "We Are Family." There was not a dry eye in the church.

I would not trade those hard days, though, because they made me lean hard on God. Looking back, I can clearly see His hand shaping every moment. I learned that when you come to the place where He is all you have, you find that He is indeed all you need. "'For I know the plans I have for you,' declares the LORD, 'plans to prosper you and not to harm you, plans to give you hope and a future'" (Jer. 29:11). He has plans for second chances, and they are good ones.

Guiding Principles

A Pinch of Salt

> We will not always understand what God is doing. His ways are not our ways, nor are His thoughts ours (Isa. 55:8).

> Tell God about all of your struggles. He truly cares about every aspect of our lives—from the loneliness to the bills that are too large to pay. Bathe yourself in His timeless Word.

> Trust God in perhaps a more unique way than ever before. Embrace Him as "the God of all comfort" (2 Cor. 1:3). Believe in His character even when you cannot possibly see how things will turn out.

> If possible, join a MOPS group if you have young children. Get involved in a Bible study that will hold you accountable. Divorce recovery groups can be valuable, but beware of those that merely allow whining and scoping out the next date.

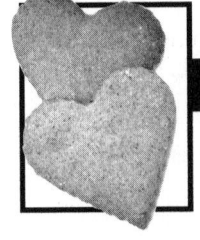

Homemade With Heart

One of Aubrey's Favorite Recipes

Two big batches of this usually take care of my family and all our guests through the whole winter. If there is anything more relaxing than curling up with a great book and a cup of this delicious hot cocoa in front of a roaring fire, I can't think of it! My girls love to come in from the snow to a big mug topped with whipped cream, miniature chocolate chips, and a candy cane.

Homemade Hot Chocolate Mix

8 qts. powdered milk
1 lb. Nesquik powder
1½ cups powdered sugar
4 Tbsp. cocoa powder
7 oz. Coffee-Mate nondairy creamer

Mix all ingredients together and store in an airtight plastic container.

To serve: Add ¼ cup of mix to a mug of very hot water. Garnish with whipped cream, cinnamon, candy canes, crushed mints, or chocolate chips. Drizzle the whipped cream with caramel or chocolate sauce for a fancy treat.

Now for an Update

With a Cherry on Top

Aubrey has been married to her wonderful husband, Eli, for nearly thirteen years. They are the parents of four beautiful daughters. Eli officially adopted Maggie, completing her long-ago prayers for a "forever family." God restored the locust years that Aubrey experienced, blessing her with a speaking and writing ministry.

Seven

Sprinkle With
the Spirit

WHETHER THEY ARE CHOCOLATE, RAINBOW, GLITTERY, or sugary pink, sprinkles lend a festive touch to the top of any birthday cake. We sprinkle confectioner's sugar on brownies; we sprinkle crumb topping on Dutch apple pie. Letting God sprinkle us with His Holy Spirit adds a spiritual dimension that is incomprehensible until it has been experienced.

When God sent Susan Hillstrom "a penny from heaven," it solidified her brand-new relationship with Him. She had been a woman scorned, and after repeated rejections, she was not about to open herself up to getting hurt again.

Just twenty-three and already a widow, Ann Smith wondered why God had allowed a horrific tragedy to overtake her. When a second heartache occurred soon after the first, she could identify with the biblical Job. In "Feeling Battered, Finding God," personal trials don't drive Ann away from God; instead, they lead to feisty conversations with Him over the years.

Jeanine Jordan did not know the Lord until the bottom fell out of her marriage and she went "searching for relationship." She explored the tenets of Christianity, and, while doing so, God showed her, in no uncertain terms, that she had His attention, and He wanted her to know it.

The Lord does that sometimes. He has a little fun with us, performing some miraculous deed that strengthens or solidifies our faith. When He sprinkles us with His Spirit, we know it unequivocally, and our lives are changed. Jesus said, "I will ask the Father, and he will give you another Counselor to be with you forever—the Spirit of truth. The world cannot accept him, because it neither sees him nor knows him. But you know him, for he lives with you and will be in you" (John 14:16–17).

A Penny From Heaven

A conversation with Susan Hillstrom

Therefore, if anyone is in Christ, he is a new creation; the
old has gone, the new has come!
—2 CORINTHIANS 5:17

"Can you come home right after work tonight?" my husband, Brian, asked. He was calling me at work and knew my habit of running errands or going to class without coming home first. Usually he would have already left for work, so it didn't matter anyway.

"I suppose I can," I answered. "What's up?"

"I'll tell you later," Brian replied. "I need to talk to you about something...it's important." He certainly sounded mysterious.

I glanced at my watch. It was three o'clock, another two hours before I could go. Brian was a policeman, and he worked the evening shift. I worked as a legal secretary during the day. I was twenty-six; he was thirty-two. We had been married for four years, but lately, because of our conflicting schedules, we didn't see much of each other. We were both independent and liked it that way.

So what could he want to talk to me about?

When I got home, Brian was standing in the kitchen. He watched me as I hung up my coat, and I could see his face was tense.

"I have bad news," he said. "I want you to hear it from me before you read it in the newspapers."

"What could he be talking about?" I wondered, and I braced myself for something awful as he walked across the room.

"You know that trip I went on last week with the guys?" he asked, looking embarrassed. "Well, I was not on a trip," he continued. "I was *with* someone, and we got caught. She is well known locally and is frequently in the public eye, which means it will hit the media any time now."

The rest of what he told me is a blur. Let's just say I did not take it very well. Multiple thoughts and emotions flooded my mind: "How long had this affair been going on? Was he sorry, or was his anger because he got caught? *How could he do this to me?*"

A girlfriend invited me to stay with her, so I moved out. I was full of anger (and had every right to be!), but at the same time, I knew I could lose everything if I wasn't careful.

I loved Brian. He was tall, handsome, and extremely charming—the adventuresome type who had a lot of friends. Brian was part of an honorable profession, and he made a decent living. We had a nice home, furniture, and cars; we even had investments in gold jewelry, diamonds, and real estate. Life was exciting. We had it all.

A few weeks later, I went back home, but no amount of pretense could get me past Brian's act of betrayal. Our relationship had changed. When I asked him to go to marriage counseling with me, he refused. We argued and fought until eventually we decided to divorce. Based on what I had learned as a legal secretary, I typed up the divorce papers myself. We agreed on the division of property and kept all the provisions amicable. I got half of our assets and the cat.

I got out of that marriage as a woman scorned who refused to look back. Within only months of the divorce, I had my own house and a new job, and I began dating. I may have been rejected, but I had a solution for that—fun! Life became a social whirl of parties and dates. A string of men and pitchers of beer numbed my aching heart.

But where was God in all this mess? I did not know, and I did not care. Church had not been a factor since I was eighteen, so I could no longer be forced to go. As far as I was concerned, religion was not for me. I was young, free, and having a good time.

Unfortunately, one of my co-workers had very different ideas about God than I did. Harriett was the only person I knew who talked about God as if He were someone real and involved in our lives. She was pretty much a Jesus freak, but she was nice.

Every Monday morning, Harriett would ask me what I had done over the weekend. I would smile and tell her all about my parties and dates, and then it was her turn to tell me what happened at her church. She talked about things like being born again and being filled with the Spirit just as easily as I talked about dancing and drinking beer.

"What do you mean, born again?" I asked her. My church upbringing had been devoid of that doctrine, so I did not understand the term. Yet Harriett seemed to personally know God, and she went on and on about how He answered her prayers.

"Do you mean to say that you talk to God?" I asked. "Can He read our thoughts and see what we do?"

"Why don't you come to the Bible study at my home?" she asked. "You will learn a lot and meet some nice people."

"No thanks!" I immediately responded. "That is not for me."

About that same time, I was playing on a coed volleyball team where I met a guy named Adam. I had been coming to practices with a casual boyfriend, but that did not keep Adam from approaching me. He seemed a little smitten with me, but he wasn't brash about it.

Adam was a down-to-earth, hard-working carpenter with solid values and a contagious smile. We were the same age, and he told me he was a Christian. "What is it with these Christians?" I wondered.

One weekend my boyfriend had to go out of town, so I gave Adam a call and we went to a movie. He was a gentleman, which I found refreshing. There was something different about him.

Meanwhile, Harriett continued befriending me at work. And after a while, I even visited her Bible study. As we studied the Bible and prayed, I noticed a great peace settle in and around me. Toward the end of the evening, Harriett's husband, a pastor, asked if he could pray for me. As he did, I began to cry—hard and deep for several minutes. I had been holding in so many hurts, and God was healing my broken heart.

After that night, I broke off relationships I was having with other men, and I dated Adam exclusively. He gave me flowers, and he even bought me my first Bible. Adam took me on picnics, invited me to meet his parents, and painted my house. Then one day he asked me to marry him! That scared me. I did not want to get my hopes up only to be rejected again.

Now I had some serious thinking to do. Adam was great, and I loved him dearly, but I didn't *want* to be born again. I liked drinking beer; I liked to party. If I became a Christian, I would have to give up all my fun! And my friends would laugh at me. My family would not understand. Above all, I did not want to be a Jesus freak.

And yet, there was a desire that would not go away—the desire to find out more about this God whom Adam and Harriett talked about. I asked every question I could think of—some of them pretty intelligent if I do say so myself. Harriett and Adam seemed to know all the answers, and they never lost their patience with me. Still I hesitated, vacillating back and forth in my mind, trying out faith like a bicycle I would ride for a while and then park at the back of the garage.

One night while talking to Adam on the phone, I realized I was ready to completely commit to God. At work the next day, I burst into Harriett's office and told her I was ready to make Jesus my Savior and Lord. I asked her if we could do it at the next Bible study, so the following Friday night, in Harriett's living room, I gave my life to Christ.

"Forgive me for everything I have done to offend You," I told the Lord. "Thank You for showing me You are real."

Again the tears flowed, eradicating emotions that I had held inside for years. A warm sensation came over me as if God was holding me in His arms. I cried cleansing, healing tears, and could not seem to stop. All the pain of rejection was being washed away, and when I left Harriett's house that night, I felt completely new.

In the days that followed, my fledgling faith began to grow. I could tell I now had a relationship with Jesus, but at the same time, I also was attacked by doubt. The healing touch that had felt so real to me in Harriett's living room seemed to recede. In its place came nagging uncertainty and questions. "What are the terms for my relationship with God?" I wondered, confused. "Could I talk to Him about everyday things, or did He only care about spiritual things? Would He care about me as an individual? Would He answer my prayers, or was that just wishful thinking?"

One day Harriett said, "Ask God for something specific and see what happens."

"I suppose I could give it a try," I responded, "but I wouldn't want something too big or too hard. It should be easy—not too taxing. Maybe I'll ask Him to give me a penny." Then in a simple, straightforward way, I asked God to send me a penny. Just one would do.

Days and then weeks went by as I watched for a penny to materialize. Would I find one lying on the sidewalk? Would I reach in for change from a vending machine and get one there? Perhaps someone with a faraway look in their eyes would hand me a penny as I wandered in the mall.

"It will come in God's good time," Harriett would chirp whenever I complained about the wait. It did not seem to faze her a bit. In fact, she seemed a little amused by the whole thing, as if she knew something I didn't. As for me, I finally gave up! This fiasco only proved that God did not care about me. Maybe the whole religion thing was a sham.

One evening I went to an aerobics workout in a school gymnasium. When class was over, I walked to the side of the gym where I had left my duffle bag. Only a few people remained in the opposite corner, engaged in quiet conversation. I was almost ready to leave when I heard a coin fall to the floor quite a distance away.

I stopped and looked in the direction of the sound. No one was there! That part of the gym was empty.

I spotted it—a penny!—and I watched as it rolled toward me with its metallic twirl. Normally a coin would roll a few feet and then stop, but this one rolled, and continued to roll, as it danced its way directly toward me. And then it stopped at my feet.

Incredulous, I stood frozen in place. I stared at that penny as it lay there silent and still. Where had it come from? There was no one in the vicinity who could have set it into play. Carefully I picked it up as if handling a sacred relic. I squeezed it to make sure it was real, and cupped it in my hand. After a long, grateful pause, I tucked the penny into my purse for safekeeping.

Adam and I started attending church together. While the pain of divorce had devastated my life, in the end it sent me reeling—with questions—toward God. It was His grace that brought me the gift of repentance and showed me a personal Jesus. As Adam and I spent hours talking about our lives and our faith, our values and beliefs merged as one. A year later, Harriett's husband officiated the ceremony at our outdoor wedding.

God had given me a second chance at marriage, and this time I had it right. He changed me with His sweet, tender love. He lifted me out of rejection and refused to condemn me. And to win me over at just the right time, God sent me a penny from heaven.

Guiding Principles

A Pinch of Salt

> ➤ Soak in as much of God as you can. Listen to Christian radio; attend church and Bible studies; read the Scriptures and do daily devotionals. You can download podcasts from online ministries and cultivate friendships with other Christians. Above all, make sure you are truly a Christian. Many people think they are Christians just because they are Americans, or because they attend church. They have not repented of their sins, and they are not trusting God to see them through life's situations. Jesus said it this way, "I am the way and the truth and the life. No one comes to the Father except through me" (John 14:6).

> ➤ Memorize Scripture verses. Harriett helped me with the first one, and it was very short: "Cast all your anxiety on him because he cares for you" (1 Pet. 5:7). This verse still has profound meaning for me. In my mind, I picture myself standing at the cross of Jesus, handing off my pain, concerns, and sins to Him. He is eager to carry our burdens if we will only trust in Him.

> ➤ Lean on God for help. The second verses I memorized were Proverbs 3:5–6: "Trust in the LORD with all your heart and lean not on your own understanding; in all your ways acknowledge him, and he will make your

paths straight." God is your only hope, and He will provide the strength you need to get through dark days.

> Start a notebook of your favorite verses, and organize it by subject. For example, if worry or fear is one of your tendencies, write down references that deal with that subject. Refer to your notebook as often as you have need, and make your concerns a matter of prayer. "Do not be anxious about anything, but in everything, by prayer and petition, with thanksgiving, present your requests to God. And the peace of God, which transcends all understanding, will guard your hearts and your minds in Christ Jesus" (Phil. 4:6–7).

> Keep a journal of your struggles, prayer requests and answers, and all the ways God is blessing you. Too often when we are in the middle of a situation, we cannot see God or how He is working. Writing on a regular basis helps us see from an eternal perspective that He is with us all the time and works everything for our good.

Homemade With Heart

One of Susan's Favorite Recipes

This is one of my husband's favorite desserts. His mother made this rich cake often, and his dad liked it so much he gave it the name, "Gentleman's Delight." My mother-in-law was kind enough to give me the recipe so I could make it for Adam and continue the tradition.

Gentleman's Delight

1 cup dates, chopped
1¾ tsp. baking soda
1½ cups boiling water
½ cup butter (softened)
1 cup sugar
2 eggs
½ tsp. salt
1 tsp. vanilla
2 cups flour
1 cup chocolate chips

Topping
⅓ cup sugar
½ cup walnuts, chopped
1 cup chocolate chips

Place dates in a small bowl and sprinkle with 1 tsp. of the baking soda. Pour boiling water over the dates. Stir and set aside.

In a large bowl, cream together the butter, sugar, eggs, salt, and vanilla. Stir the date mixture in, and then add flour, baking soda, and chocolate chips.

Pour the dough into a greased, 9 x 13 inch baking pan. Sprinkle with topping. Bake at 350°F for 40 minutes.

Now for an Update

With a Cherry on Top

Adam and Susan have been married for twenty-two years, and they adopted twin daughters as babies. Both girls have Fetal Alcohol

Spectrum Disorder but are doing well. Susan leads a small group for mothers of children with disabilities and is the editor of the disability ministry newsletter. Her passion is to know and love the Lord more completely and to tell others about the wonders of His grace.

Feeling Battered, Finding God

A conversation with Ann Smith

> Let me express my anguish. Let me be free to speak out of the bitterness of my soul.
>
> —JOB 7:11, TLB

"Mike, hurry! Hurry! Jerry is at the bottom of the pool!"

My brother-in-law ran out of the house and dove into the deep end where my husband lay motionless. I was not a strong swimmer, so I knelt at the edge to help pull him from the water. My sister-in-law, Becky, called 9-1-1 for help.

Jerry and I had met in my Ohio hometown a year after I graduated from high school. His incredible smile and gentle demeanor immediately drew me in. A few months later, on a beautiful, clear night, he proposed to me at a boat launch as the moonlight reflected a warm, romantic glow off the lake. We were convinced our relationship had been orchestrated in heaven, and the next summer we were married at the church I had attended all my life.

Jerry and I settled into a happy, early marriage routine, and we bought a house in my hometown. Three years later, he got a big promotion and was offered a transfer to New Mexico. Since I worked for the same company, they also agreed to a transfer to the new location for me.

Eager to explore our career options, we went to New Mexico for interviews, explored several possibilities for housing, and reconnected with old friends who had previously moved there. After talking it over, we decided it was a great opportunity for us. So we came back to Ohio, sold our house, packed our belongings, and headed to a new and exciting life in the Southwest.

Once we arrived, Mike and Becky, Jerry's brother and sister-in-law, opened their home to us until we were settled in our own place. On the following Monday, we would be starting our new jobs. During the next few days, we found and bought a house in Albuquerque, and I discovered that I was eight weeks pregnant!

After already knowing the disappointment of an early-term miscarriage, life was starting to take a positive turn. To me, the future looked perfect. On a Saturday night in September, just three days after we drove our U-Haul into Mike and Becky's driveway, I was sitting in their kitchen, chattering with excitement.

Then I looked out the window and noticed my five-year-old niece staring into the pool. "I wonder what Annie is looking at," I said. I went outside to join her, and that's when I saw Jerry at the bottom of the pool.

Mike worked feverishly to revive him.

"Come on, Jerry. Come on," I pleaded over and over again, hoping he could hear me. All the while, my mind was jumbled with thoughts of "Why isn't the ambulance coming? Oh please, let them hurry. Why don't I hear sirens?"

The medics finally arrived and took over. For several minutes they continued resuscitation efforts on Jerry. I was desperate to see a response—any glimmer of hope. "Jerry! Honey, can you hear me?" I pleaded as I waited for a reaction.

Finally the paramedic team lifted Jerry into the ambulance and the doors closed. My legs barely supported me as I rushed to the car where Mike was already behind the steering wheel. All the way to the hospital I repeated my plea to God, "Please don't let Jerry die…please don't let Jerry die…"

Mike followed the flashing lights and screaming sirens to the emergency room entrance. A crowd of medical personnel rushed to open the doors of the ambulance and continue lifesaving measures. They wheeled Jerry into the emergency room where the number of doctors and nurses around him grew.

A nurse ushered us to a waiting room, and I paced the floor while the clock on the wall ticked out the minutes of Jerry's struggle. After what seemed like a very long time, a solemn-looking doctor walked slowly through the door and asked to speak with me. In a somber tone he spoke the words of my fear: "I'm sorry. We did all we could."

The next thing I remember is being in the bathroom back at Mike and Becky's house. I was having a miscarriage. My girlfriend Sheila, who lived nearby, was there to help me through the ordeal. When it was over, I went out to the living room where Mike and Becky were wondering what to do. "Please call my mom and dad," I whispered, barely able to speak.

"We will be there as soon as we can get a flight," Dad said over the phone. The next morning my parents arrived in Albuquerque, and together they gripped me in a long, tight hug.

Suddenly, I was faced with the unthinkable—making arrangements for my husband's funeral. My grief was compounded by the detailed questionnaires and extensive documentation required to move a deceased person across state lines. "Dear God," I thought. "Aren't Jerry's death and the miscarriage enough? Why do I have to deal with this too?"

The agony of waiting seemed endless. It was six days later when we were able to hold the funeral in Ohio. Several hundred people came to pay their last respects. As grateful as I was in knowing they had come for my benefit too, all I could think about was how much I missed my husband.

After near-sleepless nights, I dragged through the days and weeks. We had only been married for four years, and that made me a widow before I was twenty-five! I hated being a widow. To me the word sounded old and alone.

Decisions were hard to make, and in my grief-stricken state, I had a disagreement with Jerry's mom about which of us should have some of his personal items. I kept thinking, "Why, God? Why is everything in my life going wrong? Do You not care about me at all?"

"I'm going back to New Mexico," I announced to my parents.

"Stay here," they urged. "We can send for your things. You need to be with us."

Although they were extremely supportive, I needed to find my own way in this foggy new world I had entered. I did not have my husband, I did not have our baby, and I did not have a home.

I felt as if I had nowhere to go and nothing to look forward to, so I relented and stayed in Ohio until Christmas. Then I grew restless and talked my brother into driving me to the bus station, where I bought a ticket to a small town in Iowa. Once there, I met friends who were heading west, so I rode with them to Colorado and then took a plane back to Albuquerque.

I had not kept in touch with my employer after the funeral and didn't know if I still had a job. Thankfully, it was still available. For a little while, I felt as if God had given me a small respite from tragedy and disappointment. But soon I felt battered again. Even though I did my best to fine-tune the change from a two-income household to one, the adjustment was challenging.

One afternoon as I sorted through a stack of mail, hoping there were not too many bills, I opened an envelope with an invoice for my car insurance and discovered that my rate had nearly doubled! The company had now reclassified me as a *single* woman under the age of twenty-five.

It felt as if the whole world was against me. "What are they doing?" I said aloud. "I have *been* married. It's not my fault that Jerry died."

"All right, Lord," I continued. "Now what?" It seemed as if life would always be a struggle. Though I never gave up on God, I had never fully committed to Him either.

Then one day as I drove home from work, I noticed a small sign along the road. In simple, black and red lettering, it read: "Come Join Us for Worship." The address on the sign indicated the church was only a few miles from where I lived. I knew something had been missing in my life for a long time, so I thought I would give the new church a try.

I attended a worship service the next Sunday, and the next Sunday, and the next. Every week the young pastor preached solid biblical truths in an understated but confident way that gave my life a new meaning. I never had a thunder-and-lightning moment where God showed me His presence, but I began to understand the importance of Jesus's death on the cross and how it made the way for all of us to get to heaven. I claimed many Scripture verses of reassurance for those who mourn, and I started to rely on them to help me through my daily difficulties.

The fledgling congregation grew every week, and I met many faith-filled people who were struggling like me in some way but growing in their faith. After a while, I signed up to work in the nursery and volunteered to teach Sunday school.

When I was young, I depended mostly on rote prayers that I learned as a child. Now, I talk to the Lord as if I am having a conversation with a close friend. Sometimes I sound a lot like Job in the Old Testament: "My life drags by—day after hopeless day. My life is but a breath, and nothing good is left" (Job 7:6–7, TLB). Most days I praise God for His many blessings. Over the years I have learned to trust in Him for guidance. I have also joined many of my friends at church in studying *The Purpose Driven Life*.[1] I try to focus on Christ, and as I do, He continues to bring new meaning into each day.

Why did Jerry die so young? Life's hard questions are still unresolved in my mind, but I don't demand the answers anymore. Instead, I have learned to trust God enough to rely on Him. I believe that one day, in His good timing, He will tell me everything I want to know.

Guiding Principles

A Pinch of Salt

> Force yourself to socialize, even if you are troubled or grieving. Find a group of supportive people at work, at church, or in your neighborhood. Let them minister to you as needed, and be ready to help others in return. "God has given each of you some special abilities; be sure to use them to help each other, passing on to others God's many kinds of blessings" (1 Pet. 4:10, TLB).

> Manage your money carefully. Live within your means and make sure you start a savings account. Consistently put aside some money, no matter how little, even before you pay your bills. You will feel more secure if you have an emergency fund. Then set a goal to increase the amount a little at a time.

> Talk with God even if it is just to pour out your sorrow. He will gently draw you near to Him and place right desires in your heart. He is inviting you to put Him first in your life so that He can bless you. Trust Him, and He will provide. "But seek first His kingdom and His righteousness, and all these things will be added to you" (Matt. 6:33, NAS).

> Know that God is near. "For God has said, 'I will never leave you; I will never abandon you'" (Heb. 13:5, GNT).

Homemade With Heart

One of Ann's Favorite Recipes

I am a social being who loves parties and casual neighborhood get-togethers. Banana Trifle has been a longtime favorite with my co-workers, family members, church friends, and neighborhood groups. It's easy and fun to make, and it looks very elegant when layered in a clear glass bowl.

Ever-So-Elegant Banana Trifle

1 pkg. (3 oz.) strawberry Jell-O
¾ cup boiling water
Ice cubes
¾ cup cold water
1 cup bananas, sliced
1 cup strawberries, sliced
Pound cake
¼ cup orange juice
1 pkg. (4 oz.) vanilla instant pudding (may substitute sugar free)
1½ cups cold milk
½ cup Cool Whip

Pour gelatin into boiling water and stir until dissolved. Add ice cubes to cold water to make a total of 1¼ cups. Add this cold water to the gelatin and stir until slightly thickened. Remove any unmelted ice.

Stir bananas and strawberries into the thickened gelatin.

Cut the pound cake into half-inch cubes. Place 2 cups of the cubes into a large, clear bowl. Sprinkle orange juice onto the cake cubes. Spoon the gelatin fruit mixture over the cake, and chill in the refrigerator for 15 minutes.

Prepare the pudding according to package directions, using 1½ cups cold milk. Let stand 5 minutes until thickened. Fold whipped topping into the pudding, and then spoon the pudding mixture into the bowl on top of the gelatin. Chill for at least 2 hours.

Garnish the top with strawberries and bananas.

Now for an Update

With a Cherry on Top

Ann eventually married again and spent many years with her new husband and his grown children and grandchildren. She is now a widow for a second time, but phone calls, e-mail messages, and personal visits have kept her in close contact with her Ohio family and friends; she is also a long-distance confidante to many nieces and nephews. Ann fills her life with friends, a busy job, church involvements, and feisty conversations with God.

Searching for Relationship

A conversation with Jeanine Jordan

> Have mercy on me, O God, have mercy! I look to you for
> protection. I will hide beneath the shadow of your wings
> until the danger passes by.
>
> —PSALM 57:1, NLT

The phone rang in our apartment, and the caller ID told me it was my husband. He had gone to the post office to mail our quarterly estimated taxes. I wondered what he wanted, or if he had been in an accident.

"I want a divorce," he said with a sharp edge to his voice.

What? My thoughts and words seemed to freeze. This could not be happening. He never said anything like that before. What kind of a man calls his wife on the cell phone and says that?

"What do you mean?" I asked. "I had no idea you were thinking about a divorce." For some time I had felt something was wrong. He spent countless hours locked in his office with the computer. He even slept there instead of in our bed. Besides shutting me out of his life, he became hypercritical of me about everything from what I cooked to the way I dressed and wore my hair.

He gave no further answer, just a moan of disgust.

"Can't you reconsider?" I asked. "Can't we go for counseling? I'll do anything…"

"No!" he shouted. "I have met someone else, and I want a divorce." Even after he hung up, I continued to hold the phone to my ear. "This must be a dream," I thought as my body started to tingle and my mind went numb.

Two hours later he burst through the door and slammed it behind him. "I meant what I said," he snapped and then bolted for his office.

Not wanting to feel his hatefulness, I retreated to our bedroom. If he left, what would I do? Where would I live? Our two little girls were only two and four years old. What would I tell them? I hugged myself and tried to stop my hands from shaking. "God, help me," I prayed instinctively.

Here I was, calling out to God even though I didn't know Him well. As I sat there trying to comprehend what had happened that evening, I remembered something. A few weeks ago a man had made an announcement in church about an upcoming Alpha study for people who wanted to explore or revisit the Christian faith. His words came back to me. Instead of sounding as if he had all the answers, like some Christians do, he humbly mentioned that for years he had problems in his marriage. "Those ten weeks of Alpha helped me to understand God for the first time," he said. "It also showed me the role God wants to play in my life."

At the time, I wondered if I would benefit from such a course. Now there was a new urgency as I thought, "Maybe this is what I need, what I have been looking for."

It was still two weeks until the course would begin. I counted the days, even the hours, until the designated night. Meanwhile, my husband continued his stony stalemate and made plans to permanently move out of the house.

That first night at Alpha, the crowd was larger than I expected, and I almost left. People smiled and nodded, and they didn't try to smother me. After the dinner and opening worship service, I took a seat at a table in the back of the room. I watched as the leaders introduced themselves and started the small group discussion. They seemed warm and caring, and solicited discussion from those who were braver than I. They didn't preach; they kept their remarks unbiased and brief. By the time the evening ended, I knew I would be back.

The next week we were given Bibles to take home. I had never owned a Bible, and this one had a soft, white cover. I opened its pages and sampled the clear, modern phrasing of the New Living Translation. Maybe I *could* get something out of its pages. While driving home later that night, I gently set the Bible on the seat beside me, and whenever I glanced at it, I felt a new hope stir inside.

My reverie, however, was short-lived. When I walked through the door of the apartment, my husband, who was babysitting the girls, jumped up from the couch and came toward me.

"Oh, so you're a Bible-thumper now," he taunted. "That must make you a Jesus freak." Then with a menacing tone he added, "Just remember, we have a date in divorce court tomorrow!" With that, he grabbed his leather jacket and stomped out.

The happiness I had felt while at church vanished. I rushed to the bathroom where I could be alone, and on the way past, I flung my new white Bible onto the bed.

I stayed in the restroom for several minutes, not wanting to wake the girls. When my sobbing subsided and my body was calm, I stepped out again. My Bible was laying open where I had tossed it on the bed. I picked it up, being careful not to disturb the pages, and read:

> I am worn out from sobbing. All night I flood my bed with weeping, drenching it with my tears. My vision is blurred by grief; my eyes are worn out because of all my enemies. Go away, all you who do evil, for the LORD has heard my weeping. The LORD has heard my plea; the LORD will answer my prayer.
>
> —PSALM 6:6–9, NLT

"God sees my pain!" I concluded. "He is sorry that I have to go through this, but He wants me to know He is with me."

I highlighted those verses and read them over and over. Only after I said a simple prayer to ask God for His help did I feel peaceful enough to drift off to sleep. The next morning, I took my new Bible to court and I silently directed prayers for assistance to heaven.

At one point my husband's lawyer saw the Bible clutched to my chest, and he said in a crisp voice, "You cannot bring a Bible into the courtroom."

"I can and I will," I replied. "This is going to get me through this ordeal."

I kept my Bible out on the table in plain sight during the hearing. The words of the psalm echoed in my thoughts and prayers.

During the yearlong custody battle that followed, my Bible proved an inexhaustible source of comfort. I highlighted any verse that was meaningful to me. I used sticky notes to mark passages that I would want to find again, and I slept with my Bible at night. During the ten-week Alpha course, I realized I had never taken the time to build a relationship with God. As my understanding of God grew, so did my inner calm—despite the outward turmoil of the divorce and other legal matters.

I do not want to suggest that I was without fault in the six years my husband and I were married, nor do I want to minimize the pain and rejection the divorce caused me. Yet, after that awful night when God spoke to me through the psalms, I no longer faced an uncertain future alone. He helped me function day to day, and I depended on Him for the decisions I had to make.

I returned to a career as a stylist. It was a job I was familiar with and enabled me to support my two small daughters. When my old friends first saw me there, they asked, "What's changed about you? You look so happy!" I just smiled and used the opportunity to tell them, in a gentle way, about my newfound relationship with Jesus.

God also helped me as I spoke with my daughters about our new family structure. He helped me control any fear or anger I had toward their father. I knew it was important not to taint their relationship with their dad, so I was careful of how I talked about him in their presence. All the while it was as if the Holy Spirit was saying, "I am here. I understand. I will help you."

At first I had asked God, "Why is this happening to me?" Now I focus on being thankful for all the ways He blessed me during those months of upheaval. Above everything else, I am grateful I had Him to turn to. Looking back on it, I think He used my troubled marriage and the ensuing divorce to teach me how to love and appreciate myself, other people, and most importantly, Him.

Guiding Principles

A Pinch of Salt

- Look to God's Word for comfort. "Remember your promise to me; it is my only hope. Your promise revives me; it comforts me in all my troubles" (Ps. 119:49–50, NLT).

- Spare your children, relatives, and friends diatribes about your former spouse. If you lash out with unkind words, confess it as sin. "If anyone considers himself religious and yet does not keep a tight rein on his tongue, he deceives himself and his religion is worthless" (James 1:26).

- Get involved in a good Bible study group where you can grow spiritually. Provide your children with the same opportunity.

- Remember this truth: "And we know that God causes everything to work together for the good of those who love God and are called according to his purpose for them.... He gave them right standing with himself. And having given them right standing, he gave them his glory" (Rom. 8:28, 30, NLT). We need to submit to God and trust that what we are experiencing will be used for our good.

Homemade With Heart

One of Jeanine's Favorite Recipes

When Jeanine comes home from work or school, she needs something quick for supper that the kids will like. This recipe is something a health-conscious mom can count on.

Light Waldorf Salad

1 cup celery, diced
1 cup crisp apples, diced
½ cup walnuts, coarsely chopped
½ cup seedless red grapes, halved

Dressing
½ cup unsweetened low-fat yogurt
1 Tbsp. lemon juice

Mix together celery, apples, walnuts, and grapes in a large serving bowl.

In a small bowl, mix the yogurt and lemon juice together to make dressing. Pour the dressing over the fruit and toss well. Keep refrigerated until you are ready to serve. Makes 4 servings.

Now for an Update

With a Cherry on Top

Careful to guard her fledgling faith, Jeanine took her daughters to church, stayed active in Bible study groups, and formed friendships with Christians her age. Her daughters are spectacular, she says.

Jeanine is pursuing a bachelor's degree in psychology with an emphasis in health and wellness, and she will go directly into a master's program after she graduates. She works as a personal trainer, taking pleasure in helping people achieve and maintain a healthy lifestyle.

Eight

Garnish With Grace

IF YOU ORDERED A SPECIALTY DRINK AT A COFFEE SHOP, YOU would be sorely disappointed if all you received was a cup of muddy brown water. How much more are we disappointed, disillusioned, and disgraced when we pledge our lives to another and in return receive neglect, control, and abuse. When a woman is battered physically or emotionally, she fears for her life—the life of her body and the life of her spirit.

Maggie Miller's situation had turned terribly wrong even after she tried doing everything right. Panic and fright set in when her dreams were dashed, and she wondered how a less-than-perfect outcome could still glorify God. Read how she survived and came out victorious in "Hunker Down in the Barrel, Honey."

Thoughts of suicide were on Marie Zender's mind when she could no longer cope with life. Share the details of her struggle after childhood abuse, a failed marriage, and addiction to pain killers. In this story about God's patience and grace, Marie was finally able to say, "OK, Lord, I get it."

Christine Hagion Rzepka had no parent or friend from whom to borrow courage, no neighbor or confidante to offer her a soothing cup of tea. In "Me? A Battered Woman?" she learned to stand on her own. In a desperate attempt to find a safe haven for herself and her unborn child, she stepped out and found the means to survive.

It takes grace and courage to emerge from an abusive situation and determine in your heart to use your experience to serve others. The natural response is to keep quiet, but what a blessing it can be when we dare to be transparent and minister to those still in despair.

Hunker Down in the Barrel, Honey

A conversation with Maggie Miller

> I am surprised I'm not dead or in a psych ward. But I am alive and well.
>
> —MAGGIE MILLER

At eighteen, a fairy tale danced in my imagination. I graduated from high school, packed my bags, and headed to the castle—that is, I went to a Christian college in Massachusetts to find Prince Charming.

I told myself, "He will be a pastor like my father, and I will be a pastor's wife like my mother. We will work together as a team and walk into the sunset." I rounded out my dream with visions of a tidy little house surrounded by a white picket fence, and rosy-cheeked children singing at the windows. Wouldn't life be wonderful?

So off I went, giving Mom and Dad hugs and kisses and assuring them I would be OK. "I'll study hard, write often, and let you know if I meet any cute boys," I teased.

Once at college I made plenty of friends, but I did not write home about a special guy until my senior year. That is when I met Dan, an outgoing, full-of-fun guy who was pursuing a degree in pastoral studies. We dated until graduation, and then in early summer Dan asked the question I had waited to hear. I looked at that handsome guy who was asking me to marry him, and I thought I was the luckiest girl in the world.

"Yes, yes!" I said, giddy with excitement. A few months later we were married at my father's church. But the bliss of early married life lasted only a few weeks. We had barely started our walk toward the sunset when I glimpsed Dan's *hidden* side.

As is often the case with newlyweds, we had little money and no furniture, so my parents bought us a bed. "Your parents should mind their own business," Dan said. He was insulted and infuriated.

"But we need a place to sleep," I told him as I smoothed the sheets.

"I am your husband, and I can provide for us. I don't need their help," was his reply.

I tried to understand his feelings, but my attempts to soothe his injured pride mattered little in cheering his mood. In my mind, I made a note of this surprising eruption, unaware of the thick file of observations that would accumulate as we partnered in ministry.

Dan was intent in his duties as a pastor, and thankfully he was popular with the church members. I taught Sunday school and women's Bible studies. I hosted Sunday dinners around our dining room table and took great care in making our guests feel welcome. They were interesting people, and I genuinely enjoyed engaging them in conversation. But I was careful to present the image Dan wanted as I strove for perfection in all I did.

One day when Dan came home for lunch, he announced, "We have been called to a new assignment. We will be serving a little congregation of about one hundred people." I was happy where we were. Our two little girls were born there, and I had many friends. But I was eager to follow God's leading and wanted to submit to my husband.

"When should I start packing?" I asked.

"We start next month," Dan said. And that was that.

The time passed quickly. We settled into the new congregation, and I continued to live my dream as a pastor's wife. But there was one thing I had not counted on: Dan's outbursts began to occur more often, and they escalated in intensity. The congenial image he projected at church differed sharply from the controlling personality my daughters and I lived under at home. I tried hard to "do all the right things," but his moods were unpredictable. I thought his bad temper was my fault, and I obsessed about how to be a perfect wife, run a perfect household, function as a perfect ministry partner, and project a perfect image to our congregation.

"No one must ever know the pastor's family is in turmoil," I told myself repeatedly. So I smiled and kept my mouth shut. I protected Dan. I protected our reputation. I protected the congregation.

As the pastor, Dan counseled women who came to his office. In my opinion the sessions were too frequent and lasted too long. Finally, after months of inner turmoil, I dared to ask, "Why do you spend so much time with those women?"

"They have had hard times," he answered harshly. "They need me to listen, to help and encourage them."

It didn't take long to figure out that my husband was having an affair. Still, I could hardly believe it. As crazy as it sounded, Dan and I continued to conduct marriage seminars even while our own marriage crumbled around us. "This isn't the way it's supposed to be!" I would say to God. "This is dishonest. We are hypocrites. My husband is a pastor, a marriage counselor, and people look up to him. What am I going to do?"

Weeks passed, and I could no longer stand it. I made my first major independent decision in seventeen years of marriage. One evening after I had loaded the dishwasher and cleaned up the kitchen, I faced Dan, looked him in the eye, and said, "I cannot live like this anymore. I want you to leave."

He glared at me silently for half a minute while my stomach ached and my heart pounded as I waited. I did not know what he would say. Finally, he answered with, "I'll be gone in the morning," and he left the room.

Dan moved out, but his affair soon fizzled. Afterward, he called to say he loved me and asked if he could come home, but I was not ready to take him back. The absence of tension had been a great relief, and I was enjoying the time of emotional respite.

One Sunday after church, I made a Shoofly Pie, an old favorite of mine. The girls' happy chatter kept the kitchen humming. But I looked at the empty place at the table and wondered about Dan. I did not like being a single mother. I wanted an intact family and was ready to give our marriage another chance. I couldn't be sure if I was doing the right thing, but we had been separated for four months. I called Dan that afternoon and asked him to please come home.

The separation initially made each of us fonder of the other. But in a matter of weeks our relationship got worse, not better. Things were deteriorating at the church too. My husband's relationship with the associate pastor was strained. Dan grew tired of trying to hide his moodiness, and people started seeing his true character. Friction mounted within the congregation. Eventually, he was asked to leave.

Over the next few years, we accepted several new assignments, but each time Dan built walls between himself and the church elders and congregations. Soon there were no more calls for him to work as a pastor.

"Please find a job in the secular market," I pleaded, desperate to keep up with our bills.

"I won't," he snapped back. "I am a pastor!"

"Dan, we are out of money!" I screamed, unable to comprehend his refusal to support his family in any way possible. I was too embarrassed and ashamed to face our friends and family. I was totally overwrought from the strain.

We moved to a different state, and I worked as a substitute teacher in a Christian school. The position provided food for our family, but little money was left for rent and other expenses. My stomach ached, and I slept very little. I didn't ask Dan to leave. Instead, I took the girls and left him.

"Where is God in all of this?" I wondered. "Is there any solace from a Jesus who has allowed me to endure humiliation and brokenness? Where is the God I have served all these years?" I had relied on Jesus Christ since I was twelve years old, and now reality was demanding a strong test of my faith. Even in my doubts I clung to my love of Scripture. I held on to two verses: "Consider it all joy, my brethren, when you encounter various trials, knowing that the testing of your faith produces endurance" (James 1:2–3, NASU), and, "Blessed is a man who perseveres under trial; for once he has been approved, he will receive the crown of life which the Lord has promised to those who love him" (James 1:12, NASU).

I was relieved that the girls seemed to find ways to avoid the merry-go-round of dysfunction in our household. They busied themselves with friends, reading books, or spending hours alone in their rooms. I lived like a robot in a trance, not even aware of the sexual abuse the girls endured from their father. Only years later did it come to light. I was horrified and tearfully apologized to them for my neglect. I had tried to be the mother my children needed—to trust God, to persevere—but sometimes I faltered.

From my college days on the East Coast, I remembered hearing stories of thrill seekers tucked inside a barrel and tumbling over Niagara Falls. I was no thrill seeker, but I felt as those people must have felt—falling, falling, falling with no assurance of a safe landing. I was suicidal and feared I was drowning in a river of depression.

I recalled the expression: "Hunker down in the barrel, honey, you are about to go over the falls." I hunkered down, all right. I curled into a tight little ball—with no fortitude left for even a whimper. Would I hit bottom and crash? Would I float aimlessly to the surface? Or would I be battered against the rocks and left for dead?

I sought counseling and poured out my heart. Even though I had no visible bruises, welts, or scars, my counselor looked at me with compassion in his eyes and said, "You must understand, you are an abused wife." Those words hit me with the force of a fist to the face. Tears spilled from my eyes as if a dam had broken, and I spewed out years of pent-up pressure and tension. The feeling was one of crashing headlong into rushing water and it sweeping me away.

For a while I was unable to control my direction. But there were life-lines out on that river; hands were reaching out. "Hang on, Maggie," my friends said. When I was too weak to reach back, they scooped me up and loved me.

Grateful for their care, I humbled myself and said, "I need help." They shared their homes and their food. They donated money and helped me find a job. Yes, my fairy tale had been ripped to shreds and my problems were not over, but I knew I would survive.

Could I have reached spiritual maturity with fewer trials? I would like to think so, but I decided not to second-guess God or blame Him in any way for the hardships I suffered. As happens for so many idealistic young women, the fairy-tale life I wanted never materialized. In faith I determined to look forward, not back, and for many years since those tumultuous times, God has filled my life with goodness.

Guiding Principles

A Pinch of Salt

> Remind yourself to trust God when you are tempted to step out ahead of Him and provide your own solutions to problems. I am sometimes reminded through failure that I must go to God *first* and seek Him through Scripture and prayer. "But if any of you lacks wisdom, let him ask of God, who gives to all generously and without reproach, and it will be given to him" (James 1:5, NASU).

➤ Hold on to God's promise that you can exchange doubt for faith, worry for peace of mind, tears for joy, insecurity for confidence, and disillusionment for hope. God uses every circumstance of our lives for our good. This is promised to us. "And we know that God causes all things to work together for good to those who love God, to those who are called according to His purpose" (Rom. 8:28, NASU).

➤ Accept the wise counsel and encouragement of mature friends. God urges us to "bear each other's burdens." When you feel overwhelmed and cannot think clearly, turn to friends who can help with godly advice.

Homemade With Heart

One of Maggie's Favorite Recipes

"I like to dwell on life's blessings," Maggie says. "And I have many fond childhood memories. One of those is of Shoofly Pie, a treat I liked to eat even for breakfast."

Shoofly Pie

1½ cups flour
½ cup sugar
½ tsp. nutmeg
1 tsp. cinnamon
⅓ cup butter, softened
½ cup Brer Rabbit Molasses
½ cup water
9-inch unbaked pie shell
½ tsp. baking soda

Mix flour, sugar, nutmeg, and cinnamon together in a bowl. Use a pastry blender (or a fork) to cut in butter until it is the texture of fine meal.

In another bowl, mix molasses, water, and baking soda. Pour the molasses mixture into a regular, 9-inch unbaked pie shell (it will foam up a little bit).

Sprinkle the dry mixture over the top, covering completely to the outside edges. Bake at 375°F for 35 minutes. Cool completely.

Serve at room temperature. It will be powdery on top with a tasty filling underneath. Whipped cream as a topping is optional. (This pie freezes well.)

Now for an Update

With a Cherry on Top

After Maggie left her marriage for the fourth and final time, she moved to a new city where she could support her daughters in their healing. There she began her life over too. Now through her own ministry, she helps others find their way through life's lost fairy tales. With a lively sense of humor, Maggie shares a message of hope and encouragement at seminars and women's retreats. She speaks about the reality of God's grace, compassion, and healing touch, enjoying every opportunity to tell others about the sustaining power of God's Word.

OK, Lord, I Get It

A conversation with Marie Zender

> My soul is full of trouble and my life draws near the grave.
> I am counted among those who go down to the pit; I am
> like a man without strength.
>
> —Psalm 88:3–4

The voice in my head was demanding and loud: "Put an end to this misery you call your life. You have no close friends and nothing to live for. You are hopeless!" Driving my car on the city streets, I paid no attention to the traffic or where I was going. For days I had heard similar messages playing in my head, accompanied by strong urges to kill myself and end it all.

It was May 15. I do not remember climbing into my car or driving around. All I heard were those voices saying, *"You are a nobody! Stomp on the accelerator and end it all; then you will be done. Then you will be through."*

Done is right. I was done trying to cope with things I could not fix. My heart was broken beyond repair.

I don't know how long I drove around that day. I was in a daze the whole time. When I finally pulled into a parking lot and stopped the car, I sat there just staring for a long time. After a while, I looked around, wondering, "Where am I? How did I get here?" Then I thought I recognized the plain brick building to my left. I remembered hearing that an Alcoholics Anonymous (AA) group met in that building, but I had never been inside. So I rubbed my hands across my face to wipe away the tears and, taking several panicked breaths, I walked into the building.

As I opened the door and stepped inside, a man asked, "May I help you?" I told him I was confused and desperate, and after another question or two, he directed me toward a room upstairs. An AA meeting was beginning in five minutes.

I was familiar with AA since I attended an Adult Children of Alcoholics group for ten years. Learning how to heal after an alcoholic was in control of my childhood is not an easy task. It was my father who drank more than he should have. He ruled our household with an iron hand.

Then when I was only six, my mother died. Within a year, my father married a woman who wanted *him* but did not want his three children. She treated us badly, constantly screaming and yelling, ordering us to work, work, work. With all that tension in the house, my father's abuse escalated.

At seventeen, I found my escape when I married Rick, a man I had known for three weeks. We had three children together, and as they got a little older, we took in foster children too. I loved kids, so I obtained a license that allowed us to have three foster children at a time. Over the course of eighteen years, I was a mother to nine children in addition to my three.

It didn't take long to discover that Rick, like my father, drank too much and did not treat me well. After nineteen years of marriage, Rick left the house one morning and just did not return. He let me know a few days later where he was, but otherwise cut off almost all contact. We eventually divorced.

That left me to pick up the pieces. My days as a foster mother were over, and I had to deal with the resentment of three teenagers who, for whatever reason, were not nearly as angry with their father as they were with me. Anxiety and depression became my normal fare.

Then a few years later, Bill came into my life. He was a kind and friendly man who spent his evenings at the Moose Lodge, visiting and entertaining friends with his jolly sense of humor. Everyone seemed to love and respect him, and he made me feel like a queen.

When Bill asked me to marry him, I hesitated because it was the second time I was considering marriage to a man who might be an alcoholic. "So what if he is?" I reasoned, telling myself, "I can handle it…I have had a lifetime of experience with alcoholism."

As it turned out, I could not have asked for a better husband than Bill. We were extremely compatible. He seldom drank except at the lodge, and he was not abusive. He was the partner that I wished for all my life, and we enjoyed making each other happy. For the first time, I knew what it was like to love without reservation and to be loved in return. My three children could not help but like Bill, and they respected us as a couple.

Eight years into our marriage, Bill was diagnosed with cancer of the esophagus and liver. I will never forget that terrible day because, from the start, the doctors told us there was nothing they could do. I quit my job so I could take care of him. Near the end, hospice workers came to help three times a week, and Bill was able to sleep in his own bed at home until eight days before he died.

To say I took Bill's death hard would be an understatement, and *heartbroken* does not begin to describe how I felt. The house was empty and quiet. Seldom could I think of a good reason to climb out of bed. An ominous gray cloud hovered over and around me, and I adopted the lifestyle of someone who was severely depressed.

Months went by, and I was just beginning to make some progress in dealing with my grief when my youngest son, Tony, was diagnosed with AIDS. I was extremely concerned about him, so over the next few months, I learned a great deal about his disease. But Tony continually suffered one debilitating illness after another, and less than two years later, he died.

That is when I walked away from God. Never had I been so angry and upset! Devastated by this latest in a series of losses, I hit bottom, asking God over and over again, "How can You do this to me? Not once, not twice, but, counting the divorce, three times!" I thought maybe He was punishing me for all my mistakes; maybe I *was* a real nobody, like those voices kept telling me.

Compounding my difficulties was the necessity for me to have several surgeries—five of them over the next two years. Four separate times I entered the hospital to have procedures on both of my feet at the same time. I was living alone at the time and had to take care of myself. The doctor prescribed medications for the pain, but I took them more often than I should have to combat my anxiety.

I slept as much as possible, and then I had to use the pills to sleep at night after sleeping so much during the day. This went on for months. I felt like a nothing, like I had stepped into a large pot of self-pity.

Often during those months, I entertained thoughts of suicide. But on May 15, compulsive urges took over. That's when I climbed into my car, drove through the city feeling desperate and dazed, and wound up at an AA meeting. God must have been in the driver's seat that day because it sure wasn't me. Thanks to Him, I received good counsel and averted taking my life.

The twelve steps AA uses became my lifeline for the next three years. I attended several meetings a week and formed a new set of friendships. Gradually, my self-talk improved and allowed me to push the past back where it belonged—in the past. I worked hard to change the ways I dealt with stress, so when my twenty-year-old grandson, Nathan, asked if he could live with me, it gave me just the boost I needed.

Slowly I started feeling better about myself and life in general. Then my sister Susan and a couple of girlfriends suggested that I volunteer for something. "It will help take your mind off your problems," they said.

My friend Mark had another solution. "My church is having what they call an Alpha celebration dinner," he told me one day. "I have gone to several, and it's a lot of fun. Here are two tickets. Invite a guest."

"I do not like crowds," I answered him, "and I won't know anyone there." But Mark persisted, so what else could I say? Besides, I was looking to volunteer for something anyway. Maybe going to this dinner would count.

I called my friend Marge and asked her to come with me. I had to plead with her for a while. "All right," she finally agreed. "If you go, I will go. But just this once."

That dinner proved to be a new beginning. Marge and I learned about the Alpha program and signed up for the ten-week course. When our group met in private after a meal, film, and worship, we aired our questions about Christianity along with everyone else. No one squelched, smothered, or pressured us, and long before the fifth Alpha course, we became leaders ourselves.

Marge and I invited dozens of our AA friends to Alpha, and one by one, their anger and fears were put to rest. Best of all, many of them formed a life-giving relationship with Jesus Christ. During that time, Hebrews 10:35–39 became one of my favorite passages, especially verse 39: "But we are not of those who shrink back and are destroyed, but of those who believe and are saved."

One day Marge called me. "I want to start a group at church," she said excitedly. "A twelve-step group with a Christian slant, and I need your help." We named the group Freedom Finders and arranged to meet at the church on Thursday nights. The group started out with attendance between six and fifteen people each week, and five years later it is still going strong.

Another time someone asked me to be a greeter at the Sunday morning worship services. Once again I was given an opportunity to volunteer, but I had to overcome my introverted nature—my church averages four thousand people each week.

"What did I get myself into now?" I thought as I stood trembling in the lobby at the front entrance. I checked my hair and purple velvet dress in the mirror and then positioned myself near the door.

Thrusting my hand out to each passerby felt ridiculous after a while. I tried to look enthused; my white plastic nametag and my plastic smile were a match.

Then I noticed a family of five come through the multiple doors. Dutifully, I shook hands with the mom and the dad, but in their hurry to connect with friends, the two adolescents hurried past me. Their three-year-old hung back, though, and looked up at me with a smile. "Hello. What's your name?" I asked, bending down to shake her little hand. She flung both arms around my neck and planted a big, juicy kiss on my cheek.

"OK, Lord, I get it," I mentally said to God. "You rescued me from the clutches of death and have given me many reasons to live. Bless Your holy name, Lord. Bless Your holy name."

Guiding Principles

A Pinch of Salt

> Even though you may be going through excruciating trials, believe in God and have faith. "Forget the former things; do not dwell on the past. See, I am doing a new thing! Now it springs up; do you not perceive it? I am making a way...I provide water in the desert and streams in the wasteland, to give drink to my people, my chosen, the people I formed for myself that they may proclaim my praise" (Isa. 43:18–21). God will take care of us and satisfy our deepest needs. None of us can do the job by ourselves.

> Get professional help whenever you need it. There are many wonderful programs and community resources at our disposal, including many with a biblical perspective.

› Decide to help others—it is probably one of the best ways to help yourself. When God redeems our life from the pit, how can we not tell others and pray that He will do the same for them? "Let us draw near to God with a sincere heart in full assurance of faith, having our hearts sprinkled to cleanse us from a guilty conscience and having our bodies washed with pure water. Let us hold unswervingly to the hope we profess, for he who promised is faithful. And let us consider how we may spur one another on toward love and good deeds" (Heb. 10:22–24).

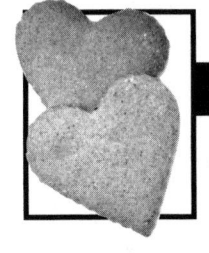

Homemade With Heart

One of Marie's Favorite Recipes

When this baked salmon fillet comes out of the oven, it looks as if a gourmet chef spent hours preparing it. Your guests will not know that it's quick and easy to make—nor will they guess the puff pastry contains only three ingredients.

I like to serve this buffet style with couscous or rice on the side. Fresh green beans or asparagus spears provide a colorful contrast to the salmon, and whole-grain dinner rolls round out the meal.

Savory Salmon Fillet

2½ pound salmon fillet
1 cup mayonnaise
1 cup grated Parmesan cheese
¼ tsp. ground red pepper (cayenne)

Wash salmon fillet thoroughly. Pat dry with a paper towel, and lay skin-side down on a cookie sheet or jelly roll pan covered with aluminum foil.

In a bowl, mix together mayonnaise, Parmesan cheese, and ground red pepper. Spread the mixture over the top and sides of the fish as if you were frosting a cake. Make a few swirls for a gourmetlike appearance.

Bake for 30 minutes at 350°F until a puffy, golden brown. Serve immediately while hot.

Now for an Update

With a Cherry on Top

Despite frail health, Marie continues to attend her church and still participates in Alpha from time to time. She keeps close tabs on Freedom Finders and is on the list of people to call if someone has a crisis.

A white cockatiel named Sam continues to be one of Marie's closest companions. He whistles "Jesus Loves Me" and greets her when she rises in the morning with, "I love you, I love you." When she leaves the room and is out of his sight, Sam calls out, "Where are you? Where are you?" until she returns. "He keeps me going," Marie says, "and in my estimation, he is yet another gift from God.

Me? A Battered Woman?

A conversation with Christine Hagion Rzepka

> He beat me when I forgot to take out the garbage. He beat
> me when I did take out the garbage. There was no right way
> to please him, so I had to leave or he would have killed me.
> —Christine Hagion Rzepka

His hands squeezed my neck and cut off the oxygen. I could not breathe. I lost consciousness, but I saw my body on the bedroom floor as if I were viewing a movie from a box seat near the ceiling. My husband had already punched me, thrown me against the wall, and kicked my swollen belly several times.

"No, no," I screamed. "Don't hurt the baby. *Please* don't hurt the baby!"

"The only way to escape this marriage is if one of us is dead," I thought. The pain no longer seared through my head, my back, and my legs. I accepted my inevitable death.

"This is my ticket out of misery," I told the Lord. "I'm ready for heaven."

I am not sure how long I hovered over my body that afternoon, but when I regained consciousness, Brad was gone and my mind was foggy. "Why am I still here?" I asked God. "Is there no end to this suffering?"

As my sensations slowly returned, I felt as if I had been pummeled by a prizefighter and then tossed in a corner to die. I could not muster enough energy to crawl to the bed. "I'm so tired," I thought. "I'll just lie here on the floor and rest. When I wake up, Lord, tell me what to do."

I fell into an exhausted sleep. When I awoke, the sun had dimmed and the apartment was still quiet. I was relieved to see that Brad had not returned. We had only been married for a few months, but already his abuse was unbearable. During my morning prayer times, I would ask God, "What am I going to do? How can I stay in this marriage?"

In the stillness, I heard God say, "You can't do anything for Me if he kills you."

This time it had gone too far! So I pushed myself to my knees and stood up, but the room swirled around me. I flopped onto the bed and wondered what to do next. I had no family to call. My father was deceased, and my alcoholic mother lived five states away. I also knew that if I called my Bible study leader, she would just insist that I stay and honor my marriage vows. And I *refused* to trust the police.

A few weeks before this incident, a neighbor overheard Brad beating me and alerted the authorities. When the officer knocked on the door, Brad opened it only as far as the chain allowed. The policeman could peer in just enough to see us. "Is everything OK here?" he asked.

I made eye contact with him and desperately shook my head, hoping for an intervention.

Smiling, Brad said, "Yes, everything is OK. We were just having an argument. You know how these women are."

"Yeah, I have one just like her at home," the policeman said. Then he turned and walked away.

Throbbing pain brought me back to the moment. Lying on the bed, I tried to plan my next step. "Now what, God?" I asked, groping for clarity. Suddenly the Child Abuse Hotline came to mind, and I grabbed for the phone. Pain stabbed my shoulder, so I reached with my other hand and called 411 to get the hotline number. It was a national holiday, but I was hoping they would answer.

"What's your emergency?" a woman's voice on the other end asked.

My pent-up fears poured out: "I am five and a half months pregnant, and my husband beat me and kicked my stomach. He tried to harm the baby. Does that qualify as child abuse?"

"Hold on for just a minute," the voice instructed. "I'm going to connect you with the battered women's shelter." The woman spoke gently while I mulled over what she said. Battered women's shelter? I didn't even know there was such a thing.

The woman then let me speak with the intake counselor, who said she would arrange a safe place for me to stay right away. Within minutes a series of cloak-and-dagger pickups and drop-offs were arranged to ensure that I would not be followed.

I called my friend Cheryl to take me to the first drop-off point. I did not know where Brad had gone, but I knew he could return at any time. I looked around the bedroom and wondered what I should take with me. I gathered a few clothes, my makeup, and my purse. Thankfully, Cheryl had agreed to store the rest of my possessions. Meanwhile, I continued to pray, "Please, God, let her get here before Brad does."

I watched through the slats of the blinds until Cheryl pulled up outside my building. I cried—not tears of relief, but tears of desperation. After spending five years as a missionary, how did my life get to be such a mess? My heart was pounding.

I opened the door to my apartment to wait, but my knees were so shaky that I could not stand. I leaned against the door frame and slid to the floor. "I am so close to freedom," I thought. "What if Brad comes home and ruins my escape?"

When Cheryl pulled up to the door, she too was worried that Brad might be nearby. She was afraid to get out of her car! Somehow I pulled myself to my feet and started gathering my things. A neighbor down the hall saw me struggling with my belongings and helped me to the car.

Cheryl drove for ten or fifteen minutes before she pulled into a parking lot where another car was waiting for me. A few minutes later I changed vehicles again. The counselor on the phone had told me that the women's shelter was under renovation and they would have to put me up at a motel for the night. So an hour after I was first picked up, the final driver delivered me to a motel. The driver stayed only long enough to make sure we had not been followed, and then she left. Now I was alone; I was scared.

"God, what do I do now?" I whispered. "Please take care of my baby, and help me to trust in You." I found a Bible in the nightstand drawer and turned to an Old Testament book. God spoke to me through the words of the prophet Isaiah:

> Fear not, for you will not be put to shame; and do not feel humiliated, for you will not be disgraced; but you will forget the shame of your youth, and the reproach of your widowhood you will remember no more. For your husband is your Maker, whose name is the LORD of hosts; and your Redeemer is the Holy One of Israel, who is called the God of all the earth....For a brief moment I forsook you, but with great compassion I will gather you.
> —ISAIAH 54:4–5, 7, NASU

Those words were my lifeline to hope. I *needed* to be gathered into God's arms and held close to His chest so I could express my fears, my exhaustion, and my isolation. I had come to the motel with little more than my life and my faith. The words in Isaiah led me to hope and comfort. God was my husband now.

I fell asleep with those words of solace. The next day I was afraid to venture out, so I stayed in my room until the staff workers came and drove me to the women's shelter. Once there, we entered a small office where an intake counselor behind the desk acknowledged my bruises and obvious pain.

"I'll try to get through these questions quickly," she said. I gave her my brief history and quietly told her that I was *not* a battered woman. But as I sat at her desk, each question I answered made that awful identity more real.

Though the counselor's questions were asked with sensitivity, tears were just under the surface of calm that I tried to present. "How far along are you?" the counselor asked.

I leaned back in the chair and rested my hand on my belly. "Five months," I replied. To my surprise, she informed me that many women are battered during their pregnancy. Then she stepped into the hallway and asked a volunteer to show me to a room. I was grateful for the short walk down a hall with no stairs to climb.

The room was a soothing shade of pink with a rose-colored blanket on the bed. Overwhelmed and exhausted, I slid under the covers and fell asleep. The following morning as I still lay in bed, I suddenly became aware of the absence of movement inside me. It was then I realized that the baby had not moved for three days!

I could not hold back my sobs. I knew the baby was dead.

I eased myself into the rocking chair near the window and crooned to my precious child. I cried off and on for a long time until no more tears would come. Then ignoring the bruises, I dropped to my knees. "If my baby is dead, Lord, bring it back to life," I prayed in desperation. "You did it for Lazarus. I am Your servant, and I know You can do it for me too."

I pulled myself up after a few more moments in prayer and slipped back under the covers for more rest. When I awoke, I felt a sharp pain. "Could it be?" I thought. Then it happened again. My baby was moving!

"Thank You, my Lord and my healer," I whispered. I cried tears of joy and pain as the baby kicked my aching ribs. I had received a personal miracle.

When I finally received long overdue medical care at the hospital, the doctors could not confirm that the baby had escaped serious injury. They observed my purple and misshapen body, my bruises and broken bones, and marveled that the baby had survived at all.

After the appointment, I was glad to return to the women's shelter for more rest. My physical healing had begun. Now I needed emotional support. It wasn't long before I was assigned to my first group therapy session.

The room we gathered in was a sanctuary of soft colors and comfortable, overstuffed chairs. We were encouraged to share the events of our lives, our beatings, and our poor choices. Boxes of tissues were plentiful. The women who had been there longer than I spoke first. But when it was my turn to share, I was embarrassed even though the others encouraged me and applauded my efforts.

I told the group about one of the times that I left Brad. I was hiding from him, and when he found me, I was in the bedroom at my sister's house. Then he asked me in a menacing voice, "Do you love your sister?" At first I didn't understand why he had asked me that.

"If you don't come home with me," he said, "I'm going to kill your sister's kids."

"Evil; you are evil," I thought. "What kind of monster can plan such hideous evil?" I could hear the kids in the next room, oblivious to any danger. "OK, OK!" I said. "You win." Brad had all the power then. I knew if he killed those children, their blood would be on my hands.

At the therapy session, heads nodded in understanding as they heard my story. It felt so good to talk when there were compassionate hearts to listen. Right then was the first time I acknowledged that I *was* a battered woman.

That therapy session, and those following it, helped me overcome feelings of defeat, shame, denial, and isolation. I wasn't alone after all.

Around the shelter, everyone helped with the cooking and cleaning. The first time I made a pan of corn bread in the kitchen, I felt giddy with freedom. Brad had often used food deprivation as a method of control. Now I could choose to eat what and when I wanted. I had begun an independent journey, and it felt good.

Before I left the shelter, someone in my group told me about Jane, a young woman who stayed in my room before I arrived. She started court proceedings in order to get custody of her children, but her abuser showed up at the courthouse. After the hearing, Jane stepped into the ladies room to regain her composure. He followed her inside and slit her throat.

My mouth dropped open. That sounded like the kind of thing Brad would do. He always threatened to track me down and kill me if I ever left him. I made an immediate decision; I would disappear.

"I'll change my name!" I thought, and it gave me a spark of hope. My entire sense of self had been destroyed by my abuser. He had degraded, mocked, and humiliated me, and he called me worthless. I also knew Brad was cunning enough to hunt for me through legal documents, so I decided against the court system. Rather than make the change legally, I would do it through usage.

Such a choice could not be taken lightly, and I wanted the assurance that God's hand was in my decision. I found my Bible and paged through the Old Testament again. Within seconds, the words of Isaiah seemed to leap off the page at me:

> You will be called by a new name that the mouth of the LORD will bestow....No longer will they call you Deserted, or name your land Desolate. But you will be called Hephzibah [meaning "my delight is in her"].
>
> —ISAIAH 62:2, 4

God was calling me holy. Not holy by my own works but because of what Christ did for me on the cross. I sensed God telling me I could change my last name to *Hagion*, which is a Greek word that means holy. In giving me a new name, God also gave me a new identity. Every time I heard my name after that, I remembered who God says I am: beloved, accepted, righteous, and blameless in His sight.

On my last day at the shelter I reflected on what I had accomplished. That first decision to pick up the phone and call for help was the key that unlocked my prison. My strength and options grew with each choice I made afterward.

From the shelter, I transitioned to a home for unwed mothers and eventually to a private residence where a married couple rented out rooms. I tried to look for a job, but not many employers would hire a single pregnant woman. So I temporarily accepted government assistance, as many abused women must do.

When the time came for my baby to be born, I changed doctors and hospitals. I did not want to take any chances that Brad would find me. An armed guard was placed outside the door of my room. On a sunny autumn day, I welcomed my beautiful little girl into the world—a world that had battered my spirit but offered hope through the hearts of compassionate people and God's living Word. My baby's tiny cry brought tears to my eyes and praise to my lips. I named her Charis, a gift of God's grace.

Guiding Principles

A Pinch of Salt

> ➤ If your husband, fiancé, or boyfriend hits, beats, kicks, or otherwise physically assaults you, you *are* a battered woman. If he is your husband, he is not upholding his marriage vows to you, and you are in danger. God does not command wives to submit to abuse. Do not delay. Call the National Domestic Violence Hotline at 1-800-799-SAFE (7233).

> ➤ Do not hesitate to take government assistance if you need it. Some people think welfare moms are lazy slobs who do drugs and don't take care of their kids. But research shows that an overwhelming majority are former victims trying to break free from a pattern of abusive relationships.

➤ No matter how frightened you may be or how alone you feel, God is there with you. He will never leave you, forsake you, or forget you. (See Hebrews 13:5; Isaiah 49:15.)

➤ Let God be your comfort and hope. Ask Him to lead and guide you through the dark times. "Trust in the LORD with all your heart; do not depend on your own understanding. Seek his will in all you do, and he will show you which path to take" (Prov. 3:5–6, NLT).

➤ Stay focused on this truth whether you are widowed, divorced, abandoned, or abused: "Thy Maker is thine husband; the LORD of hosts is his name; and thy Redeemer the Holy One of Israel; the God of the whole earth shall he be called" (Isa. 54:5, KJV).

➤ Do not give in to fear. For me, these verses were key: "No weapon formed against you shall prosper" (Isa. 54:17, NKJV); "The glory of the LORD shall be your rear guard" (Isa. 58:8, NKJV); and "For the LORD shall be thy confidence, and shall keep thy foot from being taken" (Prov. 3:26, KJV).

➤ Ask God to meet your needs, whether you need wisdom (James 1:5), protection (Ps. 107:28), provision (Matt. 6:25–33), discernment (Heb. 5:1), or courage (Josh. 1:9). We can boldly come before His Majesty, the King of kings, because we are His children. We have an open invitation to the throne room! (See Hebrews 4:16.)

Homemade With Heart

One of Christine's Favorite Recipes

I treasure the day I was able to bake corn bread at the shelter without having to ask permission from my abuser. I hope others will make the phone call that can change their lives so they too can celebrate their moment of liberation with their own batch of corn bread. I am happy to share a recipe I have named to reflect my new life.

Freedom Corn Bread

1 cup flour
1 cup cornmeal
1 Tbsp. baking powder
¼ cup honey
2 eggs
1 cup milk
½ tsp. salt
¼ cup oil or melted butter/margarine
   (If using melted butter or margarine, allow it to cool prior to mixing with the eggs.)

Preheat oven to 425°F. Grease two loaf pans or an 8 x 8 inch pan.

In a medium-sized mixing bowl, combine the first three dry ingredients. In a smaller bowl, mix together the remaining ingredients. Add the liquid mixture to the dry ingredients all at once. Stir until moistened.

Turn the batter into the prepared pan(s). Bake 20–25 minutes until a toothpick inserted in the center comes out clean.

NOTE: To make muffins, spoon the dough into greased muffin tins, filling ⅔ full. Bake for 12–15 minutes. Makes about one dozen.

Now for an Update

With a Cherry on Top

Christine is grateful for her second chance at life. For ten years she simultaneously worked and attended school before getting off welfare. Today she helps other abuse survivors start their lives over from scratch. She accompanies them to court, provides rides to apply for assistance, helps women complete their paperwork to obtain restraining orders, assists them when they move, and offers help in other areas where it is needed. She is a licensed minister and the founder and director of The Ripple Effect (www.the-ripple-effect.info), a nonprofit organization that works to prevent domestic violence. She has created a Web page on HisReach.com (a Christian alternative to MySpace.com), where you can review her profile, testimony, pictures, and blog at www.hisreach.com/revred.

Epilogue

PUT INTO PRACTICE WHAT YOU HAVE LEARNED AND WHAT the Bible says. While these stories, guiding principles, and recipes are still fresh in your mind, consider a few implications. What can we learn from the lives of these women?

1. Surrender your pain.

Only the Lord can rescue us from adversity, turning mourning into dancing and bringing wholeness where there was deficiency. Without Jesus, we are "without hope and without God in the world" (Eph. 2:12). When we yield our lives to Him, the paradigm changes and things are made new.

When we seek God's will, we are able to forgive those who have wronged us and be rid of the bitterness that festers and destroys. Surrender is a daily decision, but if we refuse to take what is offered, we will never, ever heal.

2. Persevere through suffering.

Trust that God will use your suffering to strengthen and refine you.

> Faith untried may be true faith, but it is sure to be little faith, and it is likely to remain dwarfish so long as it is without trials. Faith never prospers so well as when all things are against her; tempests are her trainers, and lightnings are her illuminators.... No flowers wear so lovely a blue as those which grow at the foot of the frozen glacier... and

no faith is so precious as that which lives and triumphs in adversity. Tried faith brings experience.... Faith increases in solidity, assurance, and intensity the more it is exercised with tribulation. Faith is precious, and its trial is precious too.[1]

—MISSIONARY CHARLES SPURGEON

Be thankful for whatever God is doing in and through your suffering, and trust that eventually He will make everything right.

3. Serve while still warm.

Good intentions quickly fade if we're not careful to serve while impassioned. Our culture distracts us at every turn. Our human nature wants to neglect serving God and our neighbor. Yet, "In the same way, faith by itself, if it is not accompanied by action, is dead" (James 2:17). Serve God through praises and prayers and by obeying His Word. Comfort others in their distress. "Each of you should look not only to your own interests, but also to the interests of others" (Phil. 2:4). "Learn to do right! Seek justice, encourage the oppressed. Defend the cause of the fatherless, plead the case of the widow" (Isa. 1:17).

Let the testimonies of the women interviewed for this book serve as powerful examples of what God can do when our faith is tested and our hearts are surrendered to Him. He enables us to endure through perilous times, and He never gives us more than we can handle. Miraculous things happen when we allow God to take our pain and transform it into a double batch of blessing.

Our prayer is that these true accounts have given you hope, strengthened your faith, and rekindled an unshakable trust in God. He sees our pain, loves us unconditionally, and waits for us to call on His name.

Notes

One
Stir With Faith

1. John and Staci Eldredge, *Captivating* (Nashville, TN: Thomas Nelson, 2005), 215.

2. *Believe!* is due for release in January 2009 (Kregel).

Two
Gather the Ingredients

1. Raymond R. Mitsch and Lynn Brookside, *Grieving the Loss of Someone You Love: Daily Meditations to Help You Through the Grieving Process* (Ventura, CA: Vine Books, 1993).

2. Dixie Johnston and Fraley Keller, *The Widow's Workbook: A Widow's Bible Study* (n.p.: Aylen Publishing, 2003).

3. Melody Beattie, *Codependent No More: How to Stop Controlling Others and Start Caring for Yourself* (Center City, MN: Hazelden Publishing, 1986).

Three
Glaze With Hope

1. Sandra P. Aldrich, *From One Single Mother to Another: Heart-Lifting Encouragement and Practical Advice*, (Ventura, CA: Gospel Light/Regal Books, 2005) Adaptation, used by permission.

2. Marie Chapian, *Making His Heart Glad*, Heart for God Series (Grand Rapids, MI: Bethany House Publishers, 1990).

Four
Marinate in Mercy

1. Lewis B. Smedes, "Arguments in Favor of Abortion Are Strong…If You Accept One All-Important Assumption," *Christianity Today*, December 2002, http://www.christianitytoday.com/ct/2002/149/57.0.html (accessed April 21, 2008).

2. Linda Joyce Heaner, *God, I Need Help* (Belleville, Ontario, Canada: Essence Publishing, 2005). Adaptation of the cemetery scene used by permission.

Five
Purée Until Peaceful

1. Nancy Markworth Brown, *Suddenly Your World Falls Apart: A Guide to Grieving Well* (Longwood, FL: Xulon Press, 2007).

2. Judson Cornwall, *Dying With Grace* (Lake Mary, FL: Charisma House, 2004).

3. Dee Brestin, *The Friendships of Women* 2nd rev. ed. (Life Journey, 2005).

Seven
Sprinkle With the Spirit

1. Rick Warren, *The Purpose Driven Life: What on Earth Am I Here For?* (Grand Rapids, MI: Zondervan, 2002).

Epilogue

1. Charles H. Spurgeon, *Morning and Evening: A Contemporary Version of a Devotional Classic Based on the NIV* (New York: Hendrickson Publishers, Inc., 1995), November 11.

Join us at Starting From Scratch!
www.StartingFromScratchBooks.com

Are you or someone you know starting from scratch? Sharon and Mary Fran host an interactive Web site with stories, a blog, inspiration, and, of course, recipes. The site also has their speaking schedule with information on how to bring them to your community.

Stop by today! We'd love to hear from you!

SHARON M. KNUDSON is a full-time freelance writer with five book collaborations and hundreds of published articles. She speaks at Christian events and retreats and also teaches writing courses on the craft of writing and getting published. She is a graduate of Christian Leaders and Speakers Services (CLASS) and holds the Toastmasters CTM award. Sharon served for four years as president of the one-hundred-thirty-member Minnesota Christian Writers Guild. She holds BME and MM degrees from Michigan State University, and lives with her husband in St. Paul, Minnesota. Visit her Web site at www.sharonknudson.com.

MARY FRAN HEITZMAN writes essays, poetry, and magazine articles, and serves as president of the Minnesota Christian Writers Guild (www.mnchristianwriters.org). She is a certified member of Toastmasters International and cofacilitates a Faith Interaction group at her church. She is also involved in the Door2Hope (www.door2hope.org) ministry at her church, which offers many services, including support for those who live with depression. Mary Fran works at Heitzman Financial Group, Inc. with her husband of thirty-seven years.